A Perfect Mess

A PERFECT MESS

*The Unlikely Ascendancy of
American Higher Education*

DAVID F. LABAREE

The University of Chicago Press
Chicago and London

The University of Chicago Press, Chicago 60637
The University of Chicago Press, Ltd., London
© 2017 by The University of Chicago
Published 2017.
Printed in the United States of America

26 25 24 23 22 21 20 19 18 17   1 2 3 4 5

ISBN-13: 978-0-226-25044-1 (cloth)
ISBN-13: 978-0-226-25058-8 (e-book)
DOI: 10.7208/chicago/9780226250588.001.0001

Library of Congress Cataloging-in-Publication Data

Names: Labaree, David F., 1947– author.
Title: A perfect mess : the unlikely ascendancy of American higher education /
David F. Labaree.
Description: Chicago : The University of Chicago Press, 2017. | Includes
bibliographical references and index.
Identifiers: LCCN 2016035743 | ISBN 9780226250441 (cloth : alk. paper) |
ISBN 9780226250588 (e-book)
Subjects: LCSH: Education, Higher—United States—History—19th century. |
Education, Higher—United States—History—20th century.
Classification: LCC LA226 .L32 2017 | DDC 378.73—dc23 LC record available
at https://lccn.loc.gov/2016035743

⊖ This paper meets the requirements of ANSI/NISO Z39.48–1992
(Permanence of Paper).

To Diane

CONTENTS

1

A SYSTEM WITHOUT A PLAN

Elements of the American Model of Higher Education

The American system of higher education is an anomaly. In the twentieth century it surged past its European forebears to become the dominant system in the world—with more money, talent, scholarly esteem, and institutional influence than any of the systems that served as its models. By all rights, this never should have happened. Its origins were remarkably humble: a loose assortment of parochial nineteenth-century liberal arts colleges, which emerged in the pursuit of sectarian expansion and civic boosterism more than scholarly distinction. These colleges had no academic credibility, no reliable source of students, and no steady funding. Yet these weaknesses of the American system in the nineteenth century turned out to be strengths in the twentieth. In the absence of strong funding and central control, individual colleges had to learn how to survive and thrive in a highly competitive market, in which they needed to rely on student tuition and alumni donations and had to develop a mode of governance that would position them to pursue any opportunity and cultivate any source of patronage. As a result, American colleges developed into an emergent system of higher education that was lean, adaptable, autonomous, consumer sensitive, self-supporting, and radically decentralized. This put the system in a strong position to expand and prosper when, before the turn of the twentieth century, it finally got what it was most grievously lacking: a surge of academic credibility (when it assumed the mantle of scientific research) and a surge of student enrollments (when it became the pipeline to the middle class). This book is an effort to understand how a system that started out so badly turned out so well—and how its apparently unworkable structure is precisely what makes the system work.

It may seem strange to call the motley collection of 4,700 American colleges and universities a system at all.[1] "System" implies a plan and a form of governance that keeps things working according to the plan; and that indeed is the formal structure of higher education systems in most countries, where a government ministry oversees the system and tinkers with it over time. The U.S. system of higher education, however, did not arise from a plan, and no agency governs it. It just happened. But it is nonetheless a system, which has a well-defined structure and a clear set of rules that guides the actions of the individuals and institutions within it.[2] In this sense, it is less like a political system guided by a constitution than a solar system guided by the laws of physics. And like the latter, its history is not a deliberate construction but an evolutionary process. The solar system also just happened, but that doesn't keep us from understanding how it came about and how it works. In this chapter, I examine the forces that drove this process of development, the distinctive structure that emerged from the process, the rules that govern the structure, and the particular benefits and costs that the structure has bestowed on this peculiarly American system. (One of the peculiarities of the system is that Americans use the terms "college" and "university" interchangeably, as I do in this book. Elsewhere in the world, "university" refers to a more elevated institution than a college, but in the United States, "college" is the default term. In the American context, using the term "university" a lot comes across as pretentious.)

To help frame this story, let me start with a few statistics. The American university, of course, has its roots in Europe; and the European university is itself one of the great institutional success stories of all time. Clark Kerr pointed this out with some dramatic numbers. By his count,

About eighty-five institutions in the Western world established by 1520 still exist in recognizable forms, with similar functions and with unbroken histories, including the Catholic church, the Parliaments of the Isle of Man, of Iceland, and of Great Britain, several Swiss cantons, and seventy universities. Kings that rule, feudal lords with vassals, and guilds with monopolies are all gone. These seventy universities, however, are still in the same locations with some of the same buildings, with professors and students doing much the same things, and with governance carried on in much the same ways.[3]

There must be something special about these institutions that gives them such incredible durability.

American universities cannot compete with their European counterparts in longevity, but they have done amazingly well in the short time they have been in existence. Consider a 2014 effort to rank the top 500 universities in the world by the Institute of Higher Education at Shanghai Jiao Tong University, using criteria like academic citations and Nobel Prizes.[4] This ranking shows that 146 of the top 500 universities in the world are American, but the proportion gets progressively higher the closer you get to the top. American universities constitute fifty-two of the top 100, thirty-two of the top fifty, and sixteen of the top twenty. Only two non-U.S. universities make it into the top ten, Cambridge and Oxford. Now one can quibble about the criteria used in this or any other ranking system, but it is hard to deny that U.S. universities, although late arrivals on the scene, have done remarkably well. Other ranking systems show a similar pattern. For example, the *Times Higher Education Supplement* rankings show the United States with fifteen of the top twenty universities.[5] Webometrics, which measures university scholarship visible on the web, shows it with seventeen out of twenty.[6] And consider another measure of eminence: between 1901 and 2013, there have been 864 Nobel laureates, and 347 of them (40 percent) were American.[7] From 2000 to 2014, 49 percent of the Nobel laureates were scholars at American universities.[8]

So what accounts for the astonishing rise by American universities in the last 100 years? One explanation is the ascendancy of the United States to a position of economic, military, and cultural dominance in the twentieth century. Wealth and power have certainly been important factors in shaping the influence of American higher education, providing this system with deep financial resources and the ability to draw a rich array of international academic talent. A second is the emergence of English as the prime international language, which has given U.S. universities an enormous advantage in reaching a world audience with its publications and in recruiting faculty and students from abroad. A third is the two world wars of the twentieth century, which devastated European (and especially German) universities while at the same time funneling large amounts of war-related research money to their protected American counterparts, and the rise of the Cold War prompted the United States to invest an enormous amount of money in university enrollments and research. As I spell out in chapter 7, all of these elements have given American universities a significant competitive advantage. In their absence, the dominance of American universities probably never would have developed.

However, I choose not to focus on these powerful contextual factors. Instead, I examine the structural elements within the system of American higher education itself that allowed this system to capitalize on the opportunities granted it by wealth, power, linguistic dominance, geographic isolation, and government investments. Without denying the importance of national might, therefore, I focus on some less obvious but equally compelling reasons for the dominance of the U.S. university. By the time all of these advantages came its way in the mid-twentieth century, the American system of higher education already had a combination of broad-based political support, large and multiple sources of revenue, institutional autonomy, and organizational capacity—all of which allowed it to make the most of the emerging historical possibilities.

To understand the success of American universities, we need to go back to a basic tension that lies at the heart of liberal democracy on both sides of the Atlantic. This is the tension between democratic politics, with its willingness to constrain liberty in order to maximize social equality, and liberal markets, with their willingness to tolerate inequality in order to maximize liberty. In higher education, this translates into a tension between social accessibility and social exclusivity, between admitting everyone and limiting access to the elite. And in both Europe and the United States, the mechanism for diffusing this tension has been the same. What allows us to accommodate both our democratic and our liberal tendencies in higher education is stratification. We can make universities both accessible and elite by creating a pyramid of institutions in which access is inclusive at the bottom and exclusive at the top. Such a system simultaneously extends opportunity and protects privilege. It offers everyone both the possibility of getting ahead through higher education and the probability of not getting ahead very far. It creates a structure in which universities are formally equal but functionally quite different, where those institutions that are most accessible provide the least social benefit, and those that are the least accessible open the most doors.

Although stratification is the generic way liberal democracies balance politics and markets in higher education, national systems differ significantly in the balance between the two sets of values. What distinguishes American universities from their European counterparts is that they are much less dependent on the state and much more responsive to market pressures from educational consumers. And the primary consequence of this market orientation is that the American system of higher education adopts a more extreme form of institutional stratification, with a markedly greater distance between the top and the bottom. The system's extended hierarchy gives a strong incentive for students, faculty, and institutions themselves to gain a place as high as possible in the structure, where the rewards are greatest. But at the same time, for all three sets of actors, the system's radical narrowing toward the top of the pyramid makes such access highly unlikely.

In the following section, I examine the way in which American higher education is organized around an educational market, fostering a kind of entrepreneurial autonomy. Then I look at how this market orientation shaped the evolution of an extraordinarily stratified system of higher education in the United States. Next I turn from

markets to politics, examining the peculiar balance of political purposes and constituencies that have shaped the system and reinforced
its broad base of support and its independence. And I compare the
American system with the medieval European university, showing
how both attained considerable autonomy by operating in the space
between the state and a countervailing force. Finally, I consider how
the American university has inherited a mixed mode of authority,
which helps reinforce its distinctive mode of organization and its ability to manage the external forces that seek to control it.

The Market-Orientation of American Higher Education

The market came late in world history, but it was there at the beginning of American history. Louis Hartz argued that the United States
skipped the feudal stage of development by being born as a liberal
society.[9] And Martin Trow developed this insight into a powerful explanation for the early emergence and stunning vitality of American
higher education.[10] Consider some of the numbers that Trow provides. Before the revolution, the American colonies had nine colleges
while the mother country had two. By the Civil War, the U.S. total
had grown to 250. "By 1910, we had nearly a thousand colleges and
universities with a third of a million students—at a time when the 16
universities in France enrolled altogether about 40,000 students."[11]

The market environment, Trow argues, fostered a peculiar kind
of organization and governance in American colleges from the very
start. Unlike their European counterparts, early American colleges
emerged as private nonprofit entities, with state corporate charters
but little or no state support. By the middle of the nineteenth century,
states had founded a number of public colleges and universities, which
quickly became the growth sector in American higher education. But
these formally public institutions also received only a portion of their
funding from government. During the twentieth century, overall state
appropriations at all public institutions of higher education fluctuated
around 20–30 percent of total revenue. The share of public university
budgets coming from state appropriations grew to a peak in the mid-

twentieth century and then has declined steadily to the present. By 2013, public institutions of higher education received about 21 percent of their funds from state appropriations, with another 16 percent from the federal government.[12]

Nowadays leading public research universities often receive less than 10 percent of their funds from the state. Most of the rest comes from donations, endowment, research grants, patents, and, most important, student tuition. A majority of these sources of revenue are independent of government control (research grants are the major exception), and pursuing them calls for a form of organization that allows, even mandates, institutions of higher education to operate like entrepreneurs in the educational marketplace. To survive and prosper, a college or university needs to be adept at attracting the tuition dollars of students and the donations of alumni. In the eighteenth and nineteenth centuries, the primary source of market-based revenue was students, and this has continued to be the case in recent years, even after other forms of income have grown substantially.

A distinctive trait of American universities is their dependence on tuition. This dependence is greater for private (mostly not-for-profit) institutions, which lack base funding from the state, but public universities also depend on tuition because of their need to supplement inadequate state subsidies and provide funds that can be spent without being subject to state guidelines. In the early to mid-twentieth century, a few states (most notably California) offered free tuition, but this experiment disappeared in the latter part of the century, as taxpayer revolts and competing fiscal demands left state appropriations lagging behind the growth in expenses. Over the course of the twentieth century, tuition fluctuated around 20–25 percent of total revenues for all institutions of higher education, and by the end of the century, tuition accounted for about 28 percent of revenues at private schools and 19 percent at public schools.[13] In 2012, students in half of the states were paying a larger share of the cost of public higher education than the state.[14]

Tuition dependence means that American colleges have always had to be nimble actors in a competitive market environment. They have to attract and retain students, position themselves in relation to competitors, adapt to changes in consumer demand and social conditions, lure contributors, and creatively pursue other forms of outside revenue. This calls for distinctive forms of governance, organization, and curriculum.

At the heart of the American model of university governance is an independent board of trustees, dominated not by government officials or academics but by laypersons. This board serves as a buffer between university and state, a counterweight to the influence of the faculty, a conduit to the real world of practical pursuits in a market society, and a source of donations. The board appoints the president, who, in the American system, is a remarkably strong figure posed against a relatively weak faculty.

A strong president, backed by a lay board, serves as the CEO of a market-oriented educational enterprise, and the structure of the institution follows suit. This means that the American system of higher education—even in the public sector—is unusually independent of the state and unusually dependent on the consumer. It also means that the system is extraordinarily stratified. Let's look at the way the stratified structure of the system developed over time.

The Result: A Highly Stratified System

A market-oriented system of higher education has a special dynamic that leads to a high degree of stratification. Each educational enterprise competes with the others to establish a position in the market that will allow it to draw students, generate a comfortable surplus, and maintain this situation over time. The problem is that, given the lack of effective state limits on the establishment and expansion of colleges, these schools find themselves in a buyer's market. Individual buyers may want one kind of program over another, which gives colleges an incentive to differentiate the market horizontally to accommodate these various demands. At the same time, however, buyers want a college diploma that will help them get ahead. This means that consumers don't just want a college education that is different; they want one that is better—better at providing access to good jobs. In response to this consumer demand, the United States has developed a multitiered hierarchy of higher education, ranging from open-access institutions at the bottom to highly exclusive institutions at the top, with each of the upper-tier institutions offering graduates a degree that provides invidious distinction over graduates from colleges in the lower tiers.

This stratified structure of higher education arose in a dynamic market system, in which the institutional actors had to operate according to four basic rules. Rule 1: Age trumps youth. It's no accident that the oldest American colleges are overrepresented in the top tier. Of the top twenty U.S. universities, nineteen were founded before 1900 and seven before 1776, even though more than half of all American universities were founded in the twentieth century.[15] Before competitors had entered the field, the oldest schools had already established a pattern of training the country's leaders, locked up access to the wealthiest families, accumulated substantial endowments, and hired the most capable faculty.

Rule 2: The strongest rewards go to those at the top of the system. This means that every college below the top has a strong incentive to move up the ladder and that top colleges have a strong incentive to preserve their advantage. Even though it is very difficult for lower-level schools to move up, this doesn't keep them from trying. Despite long odds, the possible payoff is big enough that everyone stays focused on the tier above. A few major success stories allow institutions to keep their hopes alive. University presidents lie awake at night dreaming of replicating the route to the top followed by social climbers like Berkeley, Hopkins, Chicago, and Stanford.

Rule 3: It pays to imitate your betters. When the research university emerged as the model for the top tier in American higher education in the twentieth century, it became the ideal toward which all other schools sought to move. To get ahead, you needed to offer a full array of undergraduate, graduate, and professional programs, selective admissions and professors who publish, a football stadium, and Gothic architecture. (David Riesman called this structure of imitation "the academic procession.")[16] Of course, given the advantages enjoyed by the top tier, imitation has rarely produced the desired results. But it's the only game in town. Even if you don't move up in the rankings, you at least help reassure your school's various constituencies that they are associated with something that looks like and feels like a real university.

Rule 4: It's most prudent to expand the system by creating new colleges rather than increasing enrollments at existing colleges. Periodically new waves of educational consumers push for access to higher education. Initially, existing schools expanded to meet the demand, which meant that as late as 1900 Harvard was the largest U.S. university, public or private.[17] But beyond this point in the growth process, it was not in the interest of existing institutions to provide wider access. Concerned about protecting their institutional advantage, they had no desire to sully their hard-won distinction by admitting the unwashed. Better to have this kind of thing done by additional colleges created for that purpose. The new colleges emerged, then, as a clearly designated lower tier in the system, defined as such by both their newness and their accessibility.

Think about how these rules have shaped the historical process that produced the present stratified structure of higher education. This structure has four tiers. In line with rule 1, these tiers from top to bottom emerged in roughly chronological order. The Ivy League colleges emerged in the colonial period, followed by a series of flagship state colleges in the early and mid-nineteenth century. These institutions, along with a few social climbers that emerged later, grew to form the core of the elite research universities that make up the top tier of the system. Schools in this tier are the most influential, prestigious, well-funded, exclusive, research productive, and graduate oriented—in the United States and in the world.

The second tier emerged from the land-grant colleges that began appearing in the mid- to late nineteenth century. They were created to fill a need not met by existing institutions, expanding access for a broader array of students and offering programs with practical application in areas like agriculture and engineering. They were often distinguished from the flagship research university by the word "state" in their title (as with University of Michigan vs. Michigan State University) or the label "A&M" (for "agricultural and mechanical," as with University of Texas vs. Texas A&M). But, in line with rules 2 and 3, they responded to consumer demand by quickly evolving into full-service colleges and universities, and in the twentieth century, they adopted the form and function of the research university, albeit in a more modest manner.

The third tier arose from the normal schools established in the late nineteenth century to prepare teachers. Like the land-grant schools that preceded them, these narrowly vocational institutions evolved quickly under pressure from consumers, who wanted them to model themselves after the schools in the top tiers by offering a more valuable set of credentials that would provide access to a wider array of social opportunities. Under these market pressures, normal schools evolved into teachers colleges, general-purpose state colleges, and finally, by the 1960s, comprehensive regional state universities.

The fourth tier emerged partly from the junior colleges that first arose in the early twentieth century and eventually evolved into an extensive system of community colleges. Like the land-grant college and normal school, these institutions offered access to a new set of students at a lower level of the system. Unlike their predecessors, for the most part they have not been allowed by state governments to imitate the university model, remaining primarily as two-year schools. But through the transfer option, many students use them as a more accessible route into institutions in the upper tiers.

This four-tier structure of American higher education leaves out some crucial elements of the complex American system: religious institutions and private liberal arts colleges. How do those schools fit into this picture? First, each of these institutional types occupies a particular market niche with its own parallel hierarchy, ranging from low to high status, from inclusive to exclusive. For religious schools, for example, we can easily rank the top Catholic universities (Notre Dame, Georgetown, etc.) just the way we do the best nondenominational institutions. Also, religious colleges are becoming increasingly indistinguishable from the secular private colleges, as market pressure forces them to imitate their competitors. As for liberal arts colleges, *U.S. News and World Report* has a special ranking for this sector, parallel to the ranking for national universities. To some extent, then, these two types of institutions replicate the broader hierarchy I am talking about.

Second, liberal arts colleges also often act as feeder systems into graduate programs in research universities, providing an alternative to an undergraduate university education. The name "liberal" is a proud assertion of their claim to academic prestige in an educational hierarchy where academic programs rate high and vocational programs low. Thus, although liberal arts colleges have their own hierarchy, they also claim a special place as preparatory institutions for graduate study at the top universities. In this sense they represent a high-track alternative to the low-track community college. Community colleges provide a vocationally tinged, low-cost, and easy-access way to pick up the first two years of college and then transfer to a four-year institution, whereas liberal arts colleges provide an academic, expensive, and exclusive undergraduate education and privileged access to the best graduate schools.

In this book, I write as someone who, over his career of thirty some years as a faculty member in higher ed, has taught at all levels of the system and at a wide range of institutions. While in graduate school at an Ivy (University of Pennsylvania), I taught for five years as an adjunct at a community college (Bucks County Community College) and also at a former normal school that became a comprehensive state college (Trenton State College, now called the College of New Jersey). After graduation, I taught full time for one year at a selective Catholic institution with a liberal arts focus (Georgetown University) and another year at an open-access private institution (Widener University, which had recently emerged from Pennsylvania Military College). For the next eighteen years I rose through the ranks at a former land-grant college that evolved into a public research university (Michigan State). And since 2003 I have been on the faculty at an elite private research university (Stanford). The U.S. system of higher education is astonishingly diverse and hierarchical, and my tour through some of its complexities has helped form my thinking about it.

Consider where this leaves us at the present point in our story. As a market-driven system, American higher education developed a four-tiered hierarchy of institutions. These tiers are distinguished from each other by degree of social access (greatest at the bottom) and degree of social advantage (greatest at the top). But one thing the three top tiers have in common is convergence around a single organizational ideal, the research university. Most universities end up as pale imitations of the real thing, but the ideal is remarkably attractive to institutions at all levels. Everyone wants to be Harvard.

The Broad Base of Political Support for U.S. Higher Education

But now let's turn from the educational market to look at educational politics. If one major factor that differentiates the canonical form of the university in the United States from the European model is its relative autonomy from the state and its responsiveness to the market, another is the breadth of its base of political support. Clark Kerr argues persuasively that the American university is actually a fusion of three models: the English undergraduate college, the German research university, and the American land-grant college.[18] One of the things that I think helps account for the success of the American university is not just the combination of these three elements but the balance among them. Each provides important strengths to the whole, while compensating for disadvantages brought by the others.

These three models operate in several ways to shape American higher education. In one way, they represent the tiers of the system, with the lower levels focusing on mass education of undergraduates, the top tier focusing on graduate education and scholarship, and the middle tiers focusing on practical education and applied research. In another way, however, they all can be found operating within the research universities in the top tiers.

The undergraduate college is the *populist* element. It brings in large numbers of undergraduates, who support the rest of the operation financially. In contrast with graduate students, undergraduates are more representative of the community and they pay more tuition. After graduation, they make more money than most graduate students in the arts and sciences (students in most professional schools are a different story), and then they make the largest share of donations to the university endowment. The contribution of undergraduates is more than just financial, however. It is also political. Drawing in a wide array of students from the community gives the university a broad base of political support, with large numbers of students and alumni serving as links between the public and an institution, which, without a large undergraduate program, could easily seem distant and effete. Reinforcing this populist element are the university's sports programs, which make its logo and school colors part of the regional culture.

Because of these considerations, American universities have become quite skillful at attracting undergraduates and keeping them happy. They foster, or at least tolerate, an active social life, provide a variety of athletic and cultural entertainments, establish a comfortable on-campus life style, and take care not to set up a curriculum that is too confining or standards of academic performance that are too demanding. In the American model of higher education, providing undergraduates with workout facilities, food courts, rock-climbing walls, and inflated grades is not too high a price to pay in order to support the larger university enterprise. Although this pragmatic stance toward undergraduates is a potential source of academic weakness, it is a central element of the American university's characteristic institutional strength. The key is to provide a campus experience that leads students to identify closely with the university, which becomes for them a status marker, a club membership, a web of social connections, and a badge of learning. They wear its colors with pride, promote its interests in the community, and donate generously to it as their careers advance.

The research university is the *elite* element. It focuses on establishing academic credibility for the institution at the highest level. This means hiring professors who are the most productive researchers and most esteemed scholars, attracting the most skilled graduate students, and developing the most sophisticated research facilities. All these are essential in order to provide a solid academic grounding for the university's reputation, and they are the factors that play most heavily in confirming the university's position in ranking systems. They are all that keeps many universities from being known primarily as party schools.

But these things are also enormously expensive. Research grants and patents help to allay much of the cost, but these sources are not sufficient in themselves to compensate for high salaries, low teaching loads, and high graduate-student support costs, and they tend to fluctuate unnervingly over time. A steady stream of income from tuition-paying undergraduates and professional school students helps fill the gaps and smooth the fluctuations. Plus graduates with bachelor's and professional degrees earn more and donate more than those with PhDs. A third problem is that the graduate research element of the university is potentially off-putting to the broader political base. If it were not for the institution's populist aura, arising largely from undergraduates and sports, the elite graduate university would be lacking the kind of broad public support that it has tended to enjoy in the United States, making it so that citizens think of the local university as belonging to them as much as to the academics. This helps explain that paradox that sixteen of the top twenty American party schools are research universities, including six that are ranked among the top fifty in the world.[19]

The land-grant college is the *practical* element in framing the politics of American higher education. Native to the United States (its nearest relative is the European polytechnic), it adds a crucial third ingredient to the mix by providing utility. This helps the university establish its practical relevance, its contribution to resolving public problems, its support for economic growth, and its salience as a community institution. The practical dimension helps support the enterprise, both with an infusion of contracts and grants and with a political rationale for public subsidy. It allows the university to tell the community: We are not just providing liberal undergraduate education for your children with a frosting of academic elitism; we are also providing a practical education in vocationally useful skills that will prepare students to be adept practitioners in professional roles. In addition, we are working on important practical problems in the region through our extensive efforts at applied research, which support industry and agriculture and enhance the local ecology. For example, land-grant universities have extensive systems of county-level agricultural extension agents, who apply university research to practical problems in the community (now extending well beyond help for farmers) and who act like ward leaders in a statewide political machine, drumming up popular support for the not-so-distant research university. And a smaller example: when I taught at Michigan State, I planted my lawn with Spartan Grass Seed, patented by Michigan State University. One secret to the institutional success of the American university, therefore, is the ability to shore up support for its academic activities with strong appeals to populism and practicality. Football and grass seed are as central to its success as scholarly publications.

Backstory: Roots in the European University

So far I have been focusing almost exclusively on the American university. Now I would like to provide a brief version of the backstory for this institution by exploring several elements in the history of its European predecessors. My aim is to make comparisons that might give a better picture of the workings of the American model.

The first universities in Europe emerged in the medieval period under circumstances that were unusually favorable for their ability to survive and thrive. As we have already seen, seventy of them are still in existence, so they must have been doing something right. Much of their early success derived from their ability to position themselves adroitly within the bipolar medieval world. (For this account I am drawing on Olaf Pedersen's *The First Universities*, a rich synthesis of the historical literature on the medieval origins of these institutions.)[20] There were two largely equal centers of power, wealth, and public legitimacy in medieval life—the Catholic Church and the monarchical state. The university emerged in the space between these two, an interstitial institution rather than one beholden entirely to one or the other. It used the church to protect it from the state, drawing on clerical immunities to keep civil authority from intruding on university life. It used the king and local lord to protect it from the church, drawing on state decrees and royal grants to preserve its independence from pope and bishop. At the same time, it used central authority in both church and state to protect it from local authority in each domain, asking king to limit lord and pope to limit bishop. And it exercised its own corporate powers as a medieval guild of teachers to keep both church and state at bay, through the use of the boycott (refusing to accept candidates into the guild) and the strike (refusing to teach). Poised between centers of power, able to play one against the other, the university managed to develop its own institutional structure and traditions with remarkably little interference. Thus allowed to get a good running start, the university had become largely unstoppable and indispensable by the time of the emergence of the modern nation-state.

Another book helps us pick up the story at that transition point: William Clark's *Academic Charisma and the Origins of the Research University*.[21] Clark looks at the historical development of the university in Germany from the medieval to the modern period, grounding his analysis in Max Weber's three forms of authority: traditional, rational, and charismatic.[22] He argues that the medieval university in Germany was grounded in traditional authority, with its roots in the guild of master teachers, who by tradition set the terms for admission, the curriculum, and the grounds for graduation. In the early modern period, the institution went through a process of transition that exposed it to the rational-legal demands of the emerging nation-state, making it increasingly subordinate to the state bureaucracy, which fostered a rationalized university structure that was responsive to the state's economic and political needs. Much of the story he tells is about the ways in which state control gradually intruded on the traditional form of the university and transformed professors, curriculum, students, and degrees into extensions of the utilitarian purposes of the modern state. But he also points out that charismatic authority made a reappearance in the university in the modern era in conjunction with rational authority, as the modern university came to emphasize the primacy of the individual academic author and the importance of scholarly fame in supporting the ideal of the university as a research institution.

Autonomy from Offsetting Sources of External Power: Market and State

Grounded in insights from these two works, I want to make two comparative points that may throw useful light on the situation of the American university. First, the medieval university enjoyed a remarkable degree of autonomy because of its ability to operate in the space between church and state. In the United States, as I have shown, there was also a counter to the state. It was not, however, the church but the market. Higher education here had the good fortune to arise in a setting where the market was strong, the state was weak, and the church was divided. Under these circumstances, neither church nor state could establish dominion over this emerging institution, and the market gave it the ability to operate on its own.

The market provided a powerful and effective counterforce to the state in shaping the American university—playing the same role that the church did during the founding of the university in medieval Europe. In the United States, the market has continued to serve as a powerful offset to state control. But European universities lost much of their autonomy in the early modern and modern period, as the authority of the church declined and they became increasingly subordinate to a state whose rational-legal authority grew beyond challenge. This has helped them survive, but it has limited their ability to thrive. They have been financially secure under the sponsorship of the state, which has saved them from the need to scrabble for funds in the unseemly manner of American university tuition chargers, grant getters, and donation seekers. They also have had considerable legitimacy because of the patronage of the government. These elements help explain why public universities have far greater prestige than private universities in Europe, whereas in the U.S. private institutions tend to top the rankings. (We'll see more about this issue in chapter 6.)

But this security has come at a severe cost. Limited to state funds, they have starved in comparison to the lavish finances of American universities, which can draw on multiple sources of revenue as buffers against the dips in income arising from fluctuations in state budget priorities. And European universities have had to follow the direction set by the ministry. This is in striking contrast to American universities, where more modest state appropriations place limits on state intrusion into university affairs. The result is that to a greater degree American schools are left to follow the entrepreneurial instincts of faculty, administrators, and trustees, adapting to the rhythms of the market. They adjust quickly to demands both from students seeking particular degrees and social opportunities and from industrial, political, and military customers seeking to capitalize on university research.

Autonomy from Offsetting Forms of Internal Authority: Traditional, Rational, Charismatic

The second comparative point is this: All three forms of authority— traditional, rational, and charismatic—are alive and well in the modern university and are particularly pronounced in the modern American university. A central component of the success and stability of the latter institution, I suggest, is its ability to capitalize on all three and keep them in productive balance. These elements reinforce each other in interesting ways, and they also provide countervailing sources of authority within the institution, thus preventing a single conception of the university or a single actor from winning out over others. This mixed model of governance brings another source of balance into the life of the university, akin to the role the market plays in offsetting the state.

As Clark shows, rational authority did indeed come to reshape the medieval university, and we see its effects all around us. We see elaborate structures of bureaucratic administration, businesslike budgeting mechanisms, a growing crew of professional managers, and elaborate meritocratic procedures for admitting, assessing, and advancing both students and faculty. These elements are evident in any modern university. But U.S. universities push rational authority to a higher level because of their greater dependence on the market and their need to adapt to its demands. They have to adjust the prices they charge students and the salaries they pay faculty in order to respond to the demands of their position in the stratified system of higher education, both the position they occupy and the one to which they aspire. They also need to develop elaborate research offices and development operations in order to maximize their take from grants and donations.

These structures of rational administration in the university, however, are laid over an irreducible element of traditional authority found in the guild-like mode of governance carried over from its medieval origins. We still honor the traditional rituals of collegial decision making in admitting faculty to the guild, deciding on promotion and tenure, approving curriculum, and preserving the artisanal autonomy of the classroom. We still induct students into guild apprenticeship, socialize them in arcane subjects, and grant them medieval degrees that were originally designed to measure degrees of acceptance into the guild of teachers. We put on the mason's mortarboard and clergyman's gown and engage in medieval processions for our graduation ceremonies.

These elements are common across universities in the modern era. But U.S. universities promote and preserve traditional authority in particularly exaggerated ways. Perhaps because traditions in the new world are so obviously not homegrown, they have become a mantle of medieval imagery assumed for the very modern reason of good marketing. In the late nineteenth century, the American college and university suddenly developed a passion for gothic architecture, medieval quadrangles, and invented traditions like football, homecoming, and singing the alma mater. Tradition sells in higher education, perhaps particularly so in a setting where the transplant is recent and the roots are shallow.

And then there is charisma. Some of the most engaging parts of

Clark's book are focused on the reinvigoration of charisma in the modern university. Charisma is often seen as an unstable and primitive form of authority that is peculiarly person centered (a pagan chief or an Old Testament prophet), in contrast with the solidity of tradition and the functional durability of bureaucracy. But charisma turns out to be a critically important element in the research university. Consider Weber's short-hand definition of charismatic authority: "resting on devotion to the exceptional sanctity, heroism or exemplary character of an individual person, and of the normative patterns or order revealed or ordained by him."[23] This sounds a lot like the archetype of the modern university professor, which David Lodge and Malcolm Bradbury have so brilliantly depicted in their academic satires.[24]

As Clark shows, the research university has elevated the ideal of the individual scholar. This charismatic ideal is consecrated in the organization of library catalogs and academic citations by author's name, and it is reinforced by the academic salience of fame (through the medium of awards, endowed chairs, peer referee systems, and citation indexes). It is found in the honored position of individual genius in the academic value system and embodied in the persona of the research professor. Weber considered modernity relentless and inevitable, as the forces of rationalization (i.e., the rise of rational authority over the traditional and charismatic) led to the progressive disenchantment of the world. Interestingly, however, the university is one modern organization that has managed to retain and even institutionalize some of this enchantment, by molding itself in part on medieval tradition and scholarly charisma.

Here, too, the American model of the university promotes this form of authority to a more extreme degree than its European counterparts. The academic star system fits perfectly into a market model of the university, which stratifies faculty the same way it does institutions, bidding up the pay and perks of the stars in the pursuit of individual genius and academic distinction. The ideal of the charismatic professor is like the ideal of the economic entrepreneur in American culture: both portray individuals of special ability as the bearers of progress, with institutions arising in their wake.

I am arguing, therefore, that all modern universities present a mix of these three kinds of authority, but that American universities promote each of them with greater vigor than their competitors overseas. As a result, each of these elements is more visible in the United States, and the contradictions they pose for these institutions are more apparent. In addition, the American model demonstrates the value of maintaining a dynamic balance among these conflicting visions of what a university is and how it should be run. The American research university thus has its own peculiar trinity of authorities: the father of tradition, the son of reason, and the holy ghost of charisma, with the last serving, as Clark puts it, as the ghost in the machine of the research university.[25]

Note how institutional stability and adaptability are both enhanced by this mix of authority types in the university—the ancient and the trendy, hoary tradition and current consumer preferences, rationalized procedure and personal expression. The balance of authority types within the American university serves many of the same functions as the balance between the market and the state and the balance among the populist, the elite, and the practical. In combination they all help to keep this institution from becoming too clearly defined to be flexible, from becoming too focused on one set of goals to be adaptable, and from becoming too much under the thumb of a single constituency to take advantage of the latest opportunity.[26]

So what can we learn from this understanding of the American system of higher education? In this chapter, I have focused on the organizational reasons for the success of American higher education, where success is narrowly defined as its ability to attain a dominant position internationally in institutional rankings, financial and human resources, and academic drawing power. In particular, I have looked at the peculiar balancing of tensions within the organization of the American system that allowed it to take advantage of the situation it faced in the mid-twentieth century, with growing American wealth and power. As we have seen, this mixed model of higher education has its benefits. Compared to the state model, it provides a broader base of political and economic support, more autonomy from state control, and more possibilities for pursuing new forms of knowledge and new social roles. It allows the system to expand access and increase scholarly quality at the same time, even when state support is level or falling.

Success in these terms, of course, does not come without consequences. The complexity of the American system, its emphasis on institutional autonomy, its dependence on the market, its adoption of contradictory political goals, and its governance by mixed models of organizational authority combine to produce a set of educational and social problems that I have not examined here. This structure leads to an extreme form of stratification in American higher education, which preserves social privilege at the same time that it provides social opportunity and which often puts a premium on getting ahead rather than getting an education. It allows the successes of the research university to occur at the expense of the students attending the community college and regional state university. In many ways, the top American universities are so rich and so academically distinguished largely because the institutions at the bottom are so poor and so undistinguished.

This system protects universities from overly intrusive and confining state control, but it does so by leaving them increasingly at the mercy of the consumer. They find themselves heavily dependent for survival on the whims of wealthy donors, on the fluctuating availability of research grants, and especially on a rapidly rising tide of student fees. In combination with the extreme stratification of the system, dependency on the consumer can lead to an emphasis on acquiring socially salient credentials more than gaining socially useful learning, especially at the undergraduate level. And it produces a grossly inefficient system of higher education, in which our extraordinary investment of public and private funds in the university often subsidizes private ambition more than it promotes the public good.

So it's an improbably successful system of higher education, but it has its issues. In the chapters that follow, we will explore how the system came about and what makes it work. We'll look at the creative tensions that animate it, the contradictions that complicate it, and the proposed reforms that could kill it. I could easily write this book as a critique, focusing attention on the system's failings, but instead I choose to write it as an appreciation, examining the distinctive institutional dynamics that enable it to be all things to all people. In its organizational complexity, multiple functionality, and breadth of support, the system inspires awe. So let us count the ways.

2

UNPROMISING ROOTS

The Ragtag College System in the Nineteenth Century

The roots of American higher education are extraordinarily local. Unlike the European university, with its aspirations toward universality and its history of cosmopolitanism, the American college of the nineteenth century was a hometown entity. Most often, it was founded to advance the parochial cause of promoting a particular religious denomination rather than to promote higher learning. In a setting where no church was dominant and all had to compete for visibility, stature, and congregants, founding colleges was a valuable way to plant the flag and promote the faith. This was particularly true when the population was rapidly expanding into new territories to the west, which meant that no denomination could afford to cede the new terrain to competitors. Starting a college in Ohio was a way to ensure denominational growth, prepare clergy, and spread the word.

Also, colleges were founded with an eye toward civic boosterism, intended to shore up a community's claim to be a major cultural and commercial center rather than a sleepy farm town. With a college, a town could claim that it deserved to gain lucrative recognition as a stop on the railroad line, the county seat, or even the state capital. These consequences would elevate the value of land in the town, which would work to the benefit of major landholders. In this sense, the nineteenth-century college, like much of American history, was in part the product of a land development scheme. More often than not, these two motives combined, as colleges emerged as a way to advance both the interests of particular sects and also the interests of the towns where they were lodged. Better to have multiple rationales and sources of support than just one.[1]

As a result, church officials and civic leaders around the country scrambled to get a state charter for a college, establish a board of trustees made up of local notables, and install a president. The latter (usually a clergyman) would rent a local building, hire a small and modestly accomplished faculty, and serve as the CEO of a marginal educational enterprise, which sought to draw tuition-paying students from the area in order to make the college a going concern. With colleges arising to meet local and sectarian needs, the result was the birth of a large number of small, parochial, and weakly funded institutions in a very short period of time in the nineteenth century, which meant that most of these colleges faced a difficult struggle to survive in the competition with peer institutions. Having to operate in a time and place when the market was strong, the state weak, and the church divided, these colleges found a way to get by without the kind of robust support from a national government and a national church that universities in most European countries enjoyed at the time.

In this chapter, I examine some of the consequences of the peculiarly dispersed circumstances in which American colleges had their origins. These institutions were not only geographically localized but also quite parochial in intellectual and academic stature. Quantity not quality was the driving force, and supply preceded demand. As a result, enrollments at individual institutions were small, and colleges had to drum up business every way they could. This changed when a broader societal rationale for pursuing higher education began to emerge late in the nineteenth century, arising from the German model of the research university and from middle-class demand for credentials that would provide access to the emerging white-collar occupations. At that point, finally, the system started to realize its potential, as the large number of existing colleges provided a widely distributed and fully operational infrastructure to make a huge expansion in student enrollments easy to accomplish. Only then did research begin to emerge as a central part of American colleges and universities.

Rapid Expansion and Dispersion of U.S. Colleges in the Nineteenth Century

In 1790, at the start of the first decade of the new American republic, the United States already had nineteen institutions called colleges or universities. The numbers grew gradually in the first three decades, rising to fifty by 1830, and then started accelerating. They doubled in the 1850s (reaching 250), doubled again in the following decade (563), and by 1880 totaled 811. The growth in colleges vastly exceeded the growth in population, with a total of 4.9 institutions per million population in 1790 rising to 16.1 institutions per million in 1880. As a result, the United States during the nineteenth century had by far the largest number of colleges and universities of any country in the world.[2]

By contrast, the United Kingdom started the nineteenth century with six institutions and had ten by 1880, while in France the number of universities rose from twelve to twenty-two. In all of Europe, the number of universities rose from 111 to 160 during the same period.[3] So in 1880 the United States had five times as many institutions of higher education as all of the countries in Europe combined. Why did this remarkable explosion of college expansion take place in such a short time and in such a cultural backwater?

Two governmental factors helped to foster the founding of colleges. One was a decision by the U.S. Supreme Court. In 1819, the court ruled unconstitutional an effort by the state of New Hampshire to assert control over Dartmouth College, arguing that when a state grants a charter to a public corporation it does not retain the right to meddle in the corporation's affairs. In the long view, the Dartmouth decision established the basis for American corporate law, but it had an immediate impact on the status of the liberal arts college. It confirmed that college trustees owned and governed the institution, and it protected them from state interference. If the state wanted to shape higher education, it would have to create publicly controlled institutions for this purpose instead of restructuring existing colleges that had corporate charters. This paved the way for the rise of state colleges, but it also spurred a sharp increase in the founding of private colleges, which now had legal autonomy.

The other factor that fostered college growth was a state action that didn't happen. Despite repeated efforts by supporters of the idea, the federal government never established a national university. The founding fathers favored such a move, and George Washington was particularly keen on the subject; later the Whigs picked up the cause. But it ran into a wall of opposition. The idea of founding such an institution bore the distinctive odor of aristocracy and big government, and it posed a threat to existing state public and private colleges, so a national university never materialized. If it had, however, the history of American higher ed would have taken a very different course. One university with federal backing would have been able to draw the top faculty talent and best students and would have rested on a solid financial footing. Public colleges in the states would not have been able to compete, and the marginal and parochial chartered colleges would have seemed pitiful by comparison. Instead, however, the market for corporate colleges was wide open, with no dominant actors and no state control.

Another reason for the massive number of college foundings in the United States was that the large majority of these institutions were colleges in name only, able to assert but the weakest of claims to being purveyors of higher education. In fact, they were difficult to distinguish from a variety of high schools and academies, which were also arising in abundance across the American landscape. For students, it was often a choice of going to high school or to college rather than seeing one as the feeder institution for the other. As a result, the age range of students attending high schools and colleges overlapped substantially. And some high schools offered a program of studies that was superior to the offerings at many colleges. So, for example, in 1849 the Pennsylvania legislature gave the Central High School of Philadelphia the right to offer its graduates college degrees, including the bachelor of arts and master of arts. Because it was hard for a private college to compete with a publicly funded high school, colleges tended to spring up where high schools were scarce and avoided big cities and areas like New England where high schools were common.[4]

Also these colleges were very small. Because of the dispersed and marginal nature of these institutions, it is hard to determine their size and even their number until the federal government began to collect statistics in 1870. But the figures collected by Colin Burke suggest that the average private liberal arts college (excluding the small number of state universities at the time) had an enrollment of forty-two students in 1830, rising to forty-seven in 1850.[5] This varied widely by region. New England colleges—the earliest institutions, which in turn served the largest population—had an average enrollment of 128 students in 1850, while, in the rapidly expanding educational arena of the Midwest, colleges had an average of only twenty-three students. By 1880, the average institution of higher education had 131 students.[6] In 1870, the first year for which we have data on professors, the average American college faculty had ten members, rising to fourteen in 1880.[7] The total number of degrees granted annually per college was only seventeen in both 1870 and 1880.[8]

Not only were these colleges very small, but also they were widely scattered across the countryside. Burke's survey of liberal arts colleges showed that in 1850 only 7 percent were in New England and 15 percent in the Middle Atlantic regions, the two centers of population at the time, while 28 percent were in the Southwest and 31 percent in the Midwest, the most sparsely populated sections of the country. On the face of it, this pattern of distribution is puzzling. Why put colleges so far away from concentrations of potential students?

For the most part the higher concentration of colleges in less populous areas was the result of the factors of denominational competition and civic boosterism that I have already discussed. Areas of new development were a prime opportunity for churches to establish a foothold in fresh territory and position themselves to take advantage of future growth. And the competition was fierce. Burke estimates that 87 percent of the private colleges in 1850 were denominational in origin, with 21 percent Presbyterian, 16 percent Methodist, 14 percent

Baptist, 10 percent Catholic, 8 percent Congregational, 7 percent Episcopal, and the rest scattered across seven additional denominations.[9] In addition, these remote areas were also the places where existing residents in emergent towns were desperate to attract settlers and thus where the cultural cachet of a hometown college would be seen as most advantageous. Established towns that were already economically viable did not need to set up a poor excuse for a college in order to attract residents and promote business. Overall, we need to keep in mind that colleges were not being established in response to overwhelming demand from students, whose numbers were small and whose enrollments were growing only a little more rapidly than the number of colleges seeking to lure them. Instead, the pressure was on the supply side. Colleges were being founded to meet the religious and economic needs of the founders, which helps explain both the glut of institutions and their peculiar locations.

In this sense, the nineteenth-century liberal arts college is a case in point of a much broader theme in American history. From its earliest years and well into the twentieth century, the United States has been a country with too much land and not enough buyers. The federal government was selling it cheap while also giving it away in large blocks to states, railroads, and homesteaders, which meant that every property holder became a prospective real estate speculator. The salient question was how to make your own land valuable when so much other land was available at little or no cost. As always in matters of real estate, location was everything. If you weren't on a river or railroad line, you needed something else to attract buyers. In this situation, being able to offer a school was helpful—better yet a high school, or even better still a college. Each was a way to announce that your town was a prime place to set down roots, raise a family, and start a business. Schools were featured prominently in real estate ads for imagined communities across the American West. In fact, as Matthew Kelly has shown for California, the link between schools and real estate values is a key reason for the creation of school district boundaries, to make sure that the benefits of having a school accrued to the local landowners.[10] And if your town not only had a school but also a college (proudly bearing the town's name), then it really announced itself to the world as worthy of being on the map.

One other reason for the rural bias of college founding in the United States is ideological. Republican theory has a long tradition of warning against the corrupting influences of the city. Republics need a strong community made up of hardy citizens, whose civic virtue keeps them focused on the public good and protects them from the unfettered pursuit of private gain. But the sad history of republics, from ancient Rome to the Renaissance Italian city-states, shows that the pursuit of power and wealth has tended to undermine republican community and lead to tyranny. Cities, therefore—as centers of commerce where citizens get caught up in the competition for personal gain—had to be regarded with suspicion. For this reason, the American founding fathers deliberately moved the federal capital from the two biggest cities (New York and Philadelphia) to an unpopulated swamp in Maryland where they established the District of Columbia, and states typically located their own capitals in places like Albany and Harrisburg that were in the middle of nowhere. The same logic applied to the founding of colleges. Best to put them in bucolic rural settings, far from the centers of trade and finance on the East Coast, where students would be able to develop good character and spiritual values while they pursued academic studies. This is the root of the American notion of a college campus—which was ideally marked off from its worldly surroundings by a wall, entered by a gate, presenting itself in the form of a monastic quadrangle, with a placid lawn in the middle suitable for contemplation. Most colleges in the nineteenth century were too poor to attain this ideal, but the collegiate movement at the end of the century rapidly shifted the physical layout of the college in line with that model.

Dilemmas of College Founding and Survival

The process of founding colleges in this period was akin to making sausages: better not to examine it too closely. It involved a lot of hustling, unalloyed optimism, and no little amount of dissembling. Since one major motive was denominational, few colleges were without religious affiliation. In 1834, the president of the nonsectarian University of Nashville complained: "A principal cause of the excessive multiplication and dwarfish dimensions of Western colleges is, no doubt, the diversity of religious denominations among us. Almost every sect will have its college, and generally one at least in each State. . . . Must every state be divided and subdivided into as many college associations as there are religious sects within its limits? And thus, by their mutual jealousy and distrust, effectually prevent the usefulness and prosperity of any one institution?"[11]

The other major motive for college founding was civic boosterism.[12] Consider the testimony of one of the major actors, James Sturtevant, a Yale seminary graduate who moved to the Midwest frontier where he helped found the town of Jacksonville, Illinois, and also the Congregational Illinois College located there. Looking back on the period from the end of the century with a somewhat jaundiced eye, he recalled that

> a mania of college building, which was the combined result of the prevalent speculation in land and the zeal for denominational aggrandizement, had spread all over the state. It was generally believed that one of the surest ways to promote the growth of a young city was to make it the seat of a college. It was easy to appropriate some of the best lots in the new town site to the new university, to ornament the plat with an elegant picture of the buildings "soon to be erected," and to induce the ambitious leaders of some religious body to have a college of its own, to accept a land grant, adopt the institution, and pledge to it the resources of their denomination.[13]

Then there was the never-say-die case of land speculator and college founder Jesse Fell. A leading citizen of Bloomington, Illinois, he served on the board of trustees of the newborn Illinois Wesleyan University until that institution chose to make its permanent campus in Bloomington instead of North Bloomington, where he had extensive land holdings. He promptly resigned from the board and turned his attention to attracting the new federal land-grant institution, the future University of Illinois, but this time he lost out to the town of Urbana, which was located on land owned by the Illinois Central Railroad. (Railroads in midcentury received large amounts of land in return for building rail lines, so they had a major interest in promoting towns on their property and saw college founding as a major resource in the effort.) But this didn't slow him down. Instead, he refocused his efforts toward attracting the state's first normal school, which he finally succeeded in locating in North Bloomington, which was subsequently renamed Normal. The school evolved into the present Illinois State University, which today has a dormitory named Fell Hall.[14]

Founding a college was one thing; keeping it afloat was another. If you delve into the histories of individual American colleges during the mid-nineteenth century, you find tales of woe: students rioting because of bad food, faculty salaries in arrears, no books in the library, and the poor beleaguered president trying to keep the whole shaky enterprise afloat. Take the case of Middlebury College, a Congregational institution founded in 1800, which has now become one of the premier liberal arts colleges in the country, considered one of the "little Ivies." But in 1840, when its new president arrived on campus (a Presbyterian minister named Benjamin Labaree), he found an institution that was struggling to survive, and in his twenty-five-year tenure as president, this situation did not seem to change much for the better.[15] In letters to the board of trustees, he detailed a list of woes that afflicted the small college president of his era. Hired for a salary of $1,200 a year, he found that the trustees could not afford to pay it and so he immediately set out to raise money for the college, the first of eight fund-raising campaigns that he engaged in, making a $1,000 contribution of his own and soliciting gifts from the small faculty. Money worries are the biggest theme in his letters (struggling to recruit and pay faculty, mortgaging his house to make up for his own unpaid salary, and perpetually seeking donations), but he also complained about the inevitable problems that come from trying to offer a full college curriculum with a small number of professors.

I accepted the Presidency of Middlebury College, Gentlemen, with a full understanding that your Faculty was small and that in consequence a large amount of instruction would devolve upon the President—that I should be desired to promote the financial interests of the Institution, as convenience and the duties of instruction would permit, was naturally to be expected, but I could not have anticipated that the task of relieving the College from pecuniary embarrassment, and the labor and responsibility of procuring funds for endowment for books, for buildings etc., etc. would devolve on me. Could I have foreseen what you would demand of me, I should never have engaged in your service.[16]

At one place in the correspondence he listed all of the courses he had to teach as president: "Intellectual and Moral Philosophy, Political Economy, International Law, Evidences of Christianity, History of Civilization, and Butler's Analogy."[17]

The point is that these rapidly proliferating American colleges in the nineteenth century were much more concerned about surviving than they were about attaining academic eminence. Unlike the situation in the old world, where a small number of institutions could count on the support of a strong state and a unified church, they had to scramble to acquire financial resources and social legitimacy from a motley mix of small denominations and small towns scattered across a lightly populated terrain. This does not sound like a formula for success in building a world-class system of higher education. But that, in the twentieth century, is exactly what happened. It turned out that these unimpressive origins contained central elements that enabled the system's later climb to distinction.

Sources of Promise in a Humble Collection of Colleges

By 1850, the United States had a large array of colleges that constituted a loosely defined system of higher education. Constructed without an overall plan, this system was characterized by wide geographical dispersion, radically localized governance, and the absence of guaranteed support from either church or state. Only a small number of these institutions were creatures of the individual states and dependent on state appropriations. The modal institution was the independent college in a small town with a corporate charter and stand-alone finances. Most had the blessing of a religious denomination, which granted legitimacy and a source of students but provided only modest and sporadic financial help. Instead they had to survive on the tuition paid by students and the gifts of individuals from the town and from the larger church community. Naming rights were for sale at a reasonable price. They operated in a very competitive market for higher education, where supply ran well ahead of demand and where their main selling points were that they were geographically accessible, religiously compatible, academically undemanding, and relatively inexpensive. On the latter two points, gaining admission was not a problem, flunking out was unlikely, and the cost was low enough to make it manageable for children from middle-class families with modest resources.

Already by 1850 there were other forms of higher education emerging on the American scene, including the state university, the landgrant college, and the normal school. In the next section, I discuss how these forms increased the complexity and added to the strength of the higher education system. But for now the main point is that these new forms entered a system where the basic model for the college was already established and where any newcomers would have to adapt to the same conditions that had shaped this model over the years.

At the heart of the college system was a strong and entrepreneurial president appointed by a lay board. Board members, as the trustees of the corporation, were responsible for maintaining its financial viability and, as leading citizens of the town and members of the clergy, brought the college social legitimacy and helped it solicit donations. The president (usually a clergyman) was the college's chief executive officer and, as such, had to give the school academic and spiritual credibility while at the same time maneuvering the institution through the highly competitive environment within which it had to operate. Survival was the first priority of every president, and, as we saw in the case of Middlebury College, the job involved a constant struggle to keep the institution financially afloat. This meant the president had to attract and retain credible faculty who would work cheap and to attract and retain tuition-paying students, while at the same time raising donations and teaching a large number of classes. In the absence of steady streams of funding from church or state, these colleges had to depend heavily on the tuition dollars brought in by students. This was never enough to pay all the bills, so fund-raising from the local and denominational donor constituencies was critical, and occasionally colleges would appeal for and receive funds from the state. But tuition was the bedrock on which the college's financial survival depended.

This competitive environment produced a system of colleges that by the 1850s had managed to survive if not thrive in the struggle for survival. They were lean and highly adaptable organizations, led by entrepreneurial presidents who kept a tight focus on the college's position in the market while keeping an eye peeled for potential threats and opportunities on the horizon. Presidents, trustees, and faculty knew they had to keep student-consumers happy with the educational product or they would attend college in the town down the road. Likewise, colleges had to keep the loyalty of local boosters, denominational sponsors, and alumni if they were going to maintain an ongoing flow of donations.

Building New Capacity and Complexity into the System

On this landscape of numerous and widely scattered colleges in the mid-nineteenth century grew three new kinds of institutions of higher education, which came to comprise the major sources of growth in the number of colleges and enrollments: state universities, land-grant colleges, and normal schools.

State Universities: First to arise was the state university. Initially, the distinction between public and private institutions was unclear, since all of them received corporate charters from individual states and some of the "private" ones (such as Harvard, from its earliest days in the colonial period) received state subsidies. But gradually a new kind of institution emerged, which was legally constituted under the control of state government and was not affiliated with a particular religious denomination. The first was University of Georgia, founded in 1785. There were five such universities by 1800, twelve by 1830, and twenty-one by 1860. At the latter point, twenty states had established at least one state university while fourteen others had not.[18]

These institutions received more state funds and were subject to more state control than their private counterparts, but otherwise they were not very different. Deliberately located at a distance from major population centers, they continued the pattern of geographic dispersion. Landing one of these institutions was a major plum for town fathers, and there is much lore about the chicanery that often determined which town won the prize. These state universities initially were rather small, sometimes dwarfed by the preexisting private colleges. James Axtell discovered that in 1880 only twenty-six of the 881 institutions of higher education had an enrollment of more than 200 students. "Amherst was as large as Wisconsin and Virginia, Williams was larger than Cornell and Indiana, and Bowdoin was near the size of Johns Hopkins and Minnesota. Yale, with 687 students, was much larger than Michigan, Missouri, or the City College of New York."[19]

State universities were similar to their private counterparts in another way as well. They were often the result of competitive pressures. States were reluctant to get behind in the race with other states in establishing a state university. Much like the kind of local boosterism that motivated small towns and religious denominations to support the founding of colleges, states saw the establishment of a public university as a way to support their claims to be considered an equal to their counterparts in the union, as centers of culture, commerce, and learning and as beacons of progressive public policy. Also, it helped that a state university provided a venue for doling out political patronage. For the most part, state universities developed outside New England and the Middle Atlantic states, where existing private colleges were already serving many of the same functions and effectively lobbied to head off state-subsidized competition.[20]

Land-Grant Colleges: Another form of higher education institution was arising only slightly later than the state university: the land-grant college. This uniquely American invention began as an outgrowth of efforts by the federal government to promote the sale of public lands in the new territories and states of the expanding nation. The Northwest Ordinance in 1787 set aside blocks of land in the new Northwest Territory (now the American Upper Midwest) for the support of public schools. This procedure became standard practice for new states and was extended to the support of higher education. Between 1796 and 1861, Congress made land grants for higher education to seventeen new states.[21] These grants ranged from 46,000 to 100,000 acres per state. The state was permitted to sell, lease, or donate these lands for the purpose of developing higher education. State governments frequently followed suit by donating public land to colleges instead of providing cash appropriations.

Initially the support was for higher education in general, but quickly the pattern developed that these land-grant institutions were to focus on a particular form of learning that was in support of "the useful arts." This pattern was codified in the enormously influential Morrill Land Grant Act of 1862, which specified that the proceeds of the land should be used to support such practical programs of study as agriculture, engineering, military science, and mining. Several land-grant laws followed the initial model of the Morrill Act, expanding this process of infusing resources into practical education. The number of institutions created by the Morrill Acts and their successors, not including the various land grants before 1862, totaled seventy-six.[22] Much of this money went to support existing universities, but often the money went to new land-grant schools, which signaled their practical focus by including "agricultural" or "agricultural and mechanical" in their titles.

These land-grant schools were public institutions, but they had a different orientation from the existing private colleges and state universities, whose curriculum was a traditional mix of liberal arts subjects. The new institutions sought less to prepare people for the clergy and high professions than to provide students with practical training in the skills needed to promote growth in the agricultural and industrial sectors of the economy. And outside the classroom, the faculty at these institutions focused their energies on providing support to the state's farmers and industrial enterprises—patenting inventions, solving mechanical problems, and setting up systems of agricultural extension agents throughout the state.

Normal Schools: A third group of institutions that emerged in the middle of the nineteenth century were initially more like high schools than colleges: normal schools. Although many of these were private institutions, most were established by state governments (and others by local municipalities and school districts) to prepare teachers for the public schools, driven by the rapid expansion of universal public schooling between 1830 and 1860 and the subsequent demand for new teachers. The first state normal school emerged in Massachusetts in 1839, but by 1870 there were thirty-nine and by 1880 there were seventy-six.[23] These institutions focused initially on preparing students to become elementary teachers, and their course of studies included both pedagogy and instruction in the core school subjects. They functioned as vocational high schools for teachers, and during most of the nineteenth century they were not considered institutions of higher education. As a result, their numbers are not included in the counts of such institutions that I provided earlier.

But the reason for including them here is that by the end of the century they had started evolving into colleges. By the 1890s, some of them were beginning to become teachers colleges, with the right to grant bachelor's degrees. By the 1920s and 1930s, they were beginning to drop the word "teachers" in the titles and to substitute the word "state." By the 1960s and 1970s, they were becoming regional state universities. So, for example, one such institution in Pennsylvania was founded in 1859 as Millersville State Normal School; in 1927 it became Millersville State Teachers College, in 1959 Millersville State College, and in 1983 Millersville University of Pennsylvania.[24] In 100 years of so, these institutions rose from being high schools for training teachers to regional state universities offering a comprehensive range of university degrees.

As a result of this remarkable evolution, normal schools became a central part of the American system of higher education. And their history shows how the patterns established in the mid-nineteenth century shaped the subsequent development of the system. Like their predecessors—private colleges, state universities, and land-grant colleges—they were located mostly in small towns and were scattered widely across the countryside, so they were geographically close to a large number of students. And like the others, they were the objects of contention among civic boosters seeking to attract this valuable prize. Also like the others, admission was easy and costs were low. And because their number was so large (Michigan and Minnesota had four each; California had eight), these institutions were markedly more dispersed and accessible than state universities or land-grant colleges. Like the latter two, they were state subsidized but relied on tuition, donations, and other sources of income in order to keep afloat. Their dependence on student tuition, and the consequent need to attract and retain student consumers, explains why they were so quick to move up the hierarchy to the status of university. This is what the students demanded. They saw the normal school less as a place to get trained as a teacher than as a more accessible form of higher education. As such, it would serve their purposes in opening up a broad array of social opportunities if it was able to grant college degrees, then offer programs in areas other than teaching, and eventually offer a full array of university degrees.

The System's Strengths in 1880

By 1880, the American system of higher education was extraordinarily large and spatially dispersed, with decentralized governance and a remarkable degree of institutional complexity. This system without a plan had established a distinctive structure early in the century and then elaborated on it over the succeeding decades. As noted earlier, with over 800 colleges and universities, the United States had five times as many institutions as all of the countries in Europe. They consisted of a heterogeneous array of institution types, including private denominational and nondenominational colleges, state universities, and land-grant colleges. In addition, there were seventy-six normal schools that were already on a trajectory to become colleges.

Of course, the large majority of these colleges were neither academically elevated nor large in scale. Recall that the average institution in 1880 had fourteen faculty and 123 students and granted seventeen degrees. Only twenty-six of the 811 colleges had more than 200 students. The system had enormous capacity, but only a tiny part of this capacity was being put to use. At 16.1 colleges per million of population, it is safe to say that no country in world has ever had a higher ratio of institutions of higher education to population than the United States had in 1880.[25] This was a system that was all promise and no product, but the promise was indeed extraordinary. Let me summarize the strengths that this system embodied at the moment its overcapacity was greatest and the boom era of the university was dawning.

Capacity in Place: One strength of the system was that it contained nearly all the elements needed for a rapid expansion of student enrollments. It had the necessary physical infrastructure: land, classrooms, libraries, faculty offices, administration buildings, and the rest. And this physical presence was not concentrated in a few population centers but scattered across the thinly populated landmass of a continental country. It had faculty and administration already in place, with programs of study, course offerings, and charters granting colleges the ability to award degrees. It had an established governance structure and a process for maintaining multiple streams of revenue to support the enterprise. And it had established a base of support in the local community and in the broader religious community. All it needed was students.

A Hardy Band of Survivors: Another source of strength was that this motley collection of largely undistinguished colleges and universities had succeeded in surviving a Darwinian process of natural selection in a fiercely competitive environment. Since they could not rely on steady streams of funding from church and state, they had learned to survive by hustling for dollars from prospective donors and marketing themselves to prospective students who could pay tuition. And since they were deeply rooted in isolated towns across the country, they were particularly adept at representing themselves as institutions that educated local leaders and served as cultural centers for their communities. Often the college's name contained the name of the town where it was located (Middlebury College, Millersville State Normal School), and this close identification with people and place was a major source of strength when there were so many alternatives in other towns. If they had succeeded in surviving in the mid-nineteenth century, when the number of colleges was growing so much faster than the population and funds were scarce, then they were well poised to take advantage of the coming surge of student interest, new sources of funding, and new rationales for attending college.

Consumer Sensitivity: These colleges were market-based institutions that had never enjoyed the luxury of guaranteed appropriations, so they had become adept at meeting the demands of the main constituencies in their individual markets. In particular, they had to be sensitive to what prospective students were seeking in a college experience, since these consumers were paying a major part of the bills. This meant that they did not have the ability to impose a traditional curriculum, which would be self-destructive if they sensed that students wanted something different. So when the land-grant colleges grew in popularity, other colleges quickly adopted elements of the new practical curriculum in order to keep from being squeezed out of the market. Even publicly supported institutions, such as state universities and land-grant colleges, had to be sensitive to consumers because their appropriations were often proportional to enrollment numbers. And colleges also had a strong incentive to build longstanding ties with their graduates, who would become a prime source for new students and the largest source for donations.

Adaptable Enterprises: The structure of the college—with its lay board, strong president, geographical isolation, and stand-alone finances—made it a remarkably adaptable institution. These colleges could make changes without seeking permission from the education minister or the bishop. The president was the CEO of the enterprise, and his clear mission was to maintain the viability and expand the prospects for the college. So presidents had to become adept at reading trends in the market, sensing shifts in demand, anticipating the concerns of alumni and other constituencies, and heading off threats to their mission and intrusions into their educational terrain. They had to make the most of the advantages offered to them by geography and religious affiliation and to adapt quickly to shifts in their position relative to competitors concerning such central institutional matters as program, price, and prestige. The alternative was to go out of business. Burke estimates that, between 1800 and 1850, forty liberal arts colleges closed, 17 percent of the total.[26]

A Populist Role: As I noted in the last chapter, the American university is an amalgam of the English undergraduate college, the American land-grant college, and the German research university.[27] The first two were firmly in place by 1880 and the third was on its way. The undergraduate college was the populist element, which started with the residential and rural college experience developed in Britain and added to it some distinctively American components that opened it up to a larger array of students. By locating these colleges in small towns all across the country and placing them in a competitive market that made them more concerned about survival than academic standards, the American system took on a middle-class rather than upper-class character. Poor families did not send their children to college, but ordinary middle-class families could, if they chose. Admission was easy, the academic challenge of the curriculum was moderate, and the cost of tuition was manageable. These elements created a broad popular foundation for the college that saved it, for the most part, from Oxbridge-style elitism. The college was an extension of the community and the religious denomination, a familiar local presence, a source of civic pride, and a cultural avatar representing the town to the world. Citizens did not have to have a family member connected with the school to feel that the college was theirs. This kind of populist base of support came to be enormously important when higher education enrollments started to skyrocket.

A Practical Role: Another major characteristic of the American model of higher education was its practicality. As Richard Hofstadter shows, the United States has had a long tradition of anti-intellectualism.[28] Overwhelmingly, Americans have given more attention to those who make things and make money than to those who play with ideas. Its central figures of admiration and aspiration have been inventor-engineers like Thomas Edison and self-made businessmen like Andrew Carnegie rather than academic intellectuals like William James, who were considered "European" (not a compliment). The American system of higher education, as it developed in the mid-nineteenth century, incorporated this practical orientation into the structure and function of the standard-model college. The land-grant college was both an effect and a cause of this cultural preference for usefulness. The focus on the useful arts was written into the DNA of these institutions, as an expression of the American effort to turn a college for gentlemen or intellectuals into a school for practical pursuits, with an emphasis on making things and making a living more than on gaining social polish or exploring the cultural heights. And this model, which was quite popular with consumers, spread widely to the other parts of the system. The result was not just the inclusion of subjects like engineering and applied science into the curriculum but also the orientation of the college itself as a problem solver for the businessmen and policy makers in the community. The message was: "This is your college, working for you. We produce the engineers who design your bridges, the teachers who teach your children, and the farmers who produce your food. We develop better construction methods, better schoolbooks, and better crops." So in addition to the system's broad populist base of support, there was also a practical rationale that made the system of higher education a valued contributor to the community, which earned support even from people whose children were never going to enroll in it.

The Pieces Come Together with the
Emergence of the Research University

When the German research university burst onto the American educational scene in the 1880s, the last piece of Kerr's three-part vision of American higher education fell into place. In this emerging model, the university was a place that produced cutting-edge scientific research and that provided graduate-level training for the intellectual elite. This supplied a path out of the doldrums that had settled on the once vibrant university structure in Europe, which had become irrelevant as major scientific work was being done elsewhere. And American scholars started flocking to Germany to acquire the union card of the new research-oriented scholar, the doctorate in philosophy, and to learn about the elements of the German model for transport back to the states. Johns Hopkins University, founded in 1876, was the first American institution designed around this model, but other newcomers quickly followed (Chicago, Clark, Stanford), and the existing institutions scrambled to adapt.

The new research model gave the institutionally overbuilt and academically underwhelming American system of higher education an infusion of scholarly credibility, which it had been so clearly lacking. For the first time, the system could begin to make the claim of being the locus of learning at the highest level. At the same time, colleges received a large influx of enrollments, which remedied another problem with the old model—the chronic shortage of students.

In the next chapter I explore the causes and effects of the rise of the research university at the turn of the century. I also show how the American system adopted the elements of the German model that served its needs while discarding the rest, thus complicating and rounding out the system rather than transforming it. The veneer of research made the college more respectable, while the core elements of the peculiar nineteenth-century structure of American higher education provided key sources of strength for the system, allowing it to enter the twentieth century with a roar.

3

ADDING THE PINNACLE AND
KEEPING THE BASE

The Graduate School Crowns the System, 1880–1910

The situation of American higher education in 1880 brought great opportunity but also great risk. The system had an enormous amount of excess capacity: all of those buildings and professors and programs to maintain with a thin and uncertain stream of revenue. Lacking reliable funding from church and state, it was heavily dependent on students. Yet, although enrollments were growing, there were not nearly enough students available to support the nine hundred or so colleges and proto-colleges that were in existence at the time. In addition, whereas the higher education system had broad support as an institution that was both popular and practical, it was lacking in the one thing that would distinguish it from other popular and practical institutions such as museums and trade schools and apprenticeship programs—namely, academic credibility. There were too many colleges for more than a tiny number of them to be academically distinguished (Harvard, Yale, and a few others), they were too small to hold a credible concentration of academic talent, and they were too widely dispersed across the countryside to create viable cultural communities of high intellectual caliber.

The German model of the graduate-oriented research university offered help with a critical part of this problem. In short, it offered a way to put the "higher" into American higher education. It gave a parochial, benighted, and dispersed array of colleges and universities a way to attain some degree of credibility as institutions of advanced academic learning. Its professors would come to have the new scientific degree, the PhD, which certified their position at the cutting edge of academic attainment, and they would be evaluated based on their own research productivity. Its graduate schools would draw the best-educated and most talented students in the country and induct them into the scientific methods of research and the habits of mind that would lead to authoritative scholarly publication. For the heterogeneous and barely academic structure of American higher education of 1880, the German model offered the chance to attain serious academic standing in the community and even the world.

The German research ideal gave hope for the American system, but it also posed a number of problems. The model envisioned a university that was extraordinarily elite academically and radically more expensive per student than anything that had existed before in the United States. To pursue this approach in the unalloyed fashion that German universities were doing was impossible in the American system. The German approach called for strong state support, since small and elite graduate programs would otherwise lack both the flow of funds and the political legitimacy needed to keep them going. This would not work in the American setting, where state investment in higher education still paid only a fraction of the total cost and where student tuition was essential for survival.

So instead of adopting the German model, the American system of higher education incorporated a version of it within the existing structure. The most ambitious, best financed, and oldest institutions—spurred by competitive pressure from research-oriented newcomers like Hopkins and Chicago—sought to establish major elements of the new model: organizing graduate schools, hiring professors with PhDs, developing advanced graduate programs, recruiting academically talented graduate students, and shifting faculty incentives toward the production of research. But they did this without abandoning the elements of the existing model that were critically important if they were going to be able to survive and thrive within the market-based political economy of American higher education. And they were aided in this effort by a development that had little to do with the graduate university but a lot to do with the sudden surge in student interest in enrolling in an undergraduate program.

By the 1890s, going to college started to became de rigueur for upper-middle-class American families. One factor was the sharp decline of small business and the sudden rise of managerial work in the new corporate economy, which meant that families of a certain means were unable to pass on social advantage directly to their children by having them take over the family business; instead they increasingly had to provide their children with educational credentials that would give them priority access to the new white-collar workforce. Another factor was the rapid increase in high school enrollment in the 1880s, which meant that the middle-class families that had relied on a high school education as a form of distinction began to look to college as a way to mark themselves off from the incoming horde of high school students. And a third factor was the glut of institutions in the higher education system, which meant that colleges were desperately looking for ways to attract students. So in the 1880s American colleges and universities invented most of the familiar elements the twentieth-century American undergraduate college experience that made attending college attractive to so many students (or copied them from peers): fraternities and sororities, football, comfortable dormitories, and grassy campuses adorned with medieval quadrangles in a faux gothic style. It was a mix that said: this is a place where you can meet the right people, acquire the right knowledge and skills, walk away with a useful credential, enjoy social life in a comfortable middle-class style, and do all this in a setting adorned with newly created social traditions and imported adornments from the great universities of the old country.

The large infusion of tuition-paying undergraduates reinforced the populist role that the American college had long played. Now attending college was both attractive and useful for large numbers of young middle-class men and women. This sharp increase in student enrollments brought an equally sharp increase in tuition revenues, and the closer loyalty to alma mater engendered by the new all-inclusive college lifestyle made graduates into an increasingly reliable and wealthy source of future donations for the institution. All this new money helped to subsidize the growing graduate programs and increasingly expensive research-oriented faculty. The undergraduates supported the elite academic enterprise that now allowed the college to call itself a research university. And the growth of research and graduate programs gave the institution the academic credibility it needed to offset what otherwise would have been little more than a party school for socially qualified but academically challenged undergraduates. And on top of these elements—the populist and the elite—was the continuation of the college's practical functions, serving business and society through applied research and the production of the higher end of the workforce.

But let's go back to 1880 when all of these changes began to take place and try to figure out why and how the system made its sudden transition into what by 1910 looked a lot like the modern structure of American higher education. We need to consider the situation facing the three major actors in the change: colleges, students, and employers. The revitalization of the system would not have happened unless colleges had made major changes in form and content, students had responded to these changes by pouring through the doors in large numbers, and employers had welcomed college graduates as prospective managers in burgeoning corporate bureaucracies.

First, what was the situation facing existing colleges and universities that spurred them to embrace change? And why did these changes incorporate two contradictory visions of the university—the academic ideal of graduate study and scientific research, combined with the social ideal of a vibrant undergraduate college life and an extensive extracurriculum? Second, why did middle-class families suddenly come to see college enrollment as an essential rather than frivolous pursuit? And why did middle-class youths embrace the role of college student with such enthusiasm after having found it so unattractive for most of the nineteenth century? More broadly, how did college emerge from its position of longtime marginality to become a central part of American popular culture? Third, why did corporations come to value and recruit college graduates for administrative positions? For years business leaders had scorned college men as dilettantes and book learners, who were thereby disqualified for practical work, instead preferring to hire men with little formal education at low-level jobs so they could learn the business from the ground up, from factory floor to the manager's office. Why the sudden turnabout in the way business viewed college?

The System's Structure Evolves

As we saw in the last chapter, the American system of higher education in the middle of the nineteenth century was in bad shape—with too many colleges, not enough students, and no academic credibility. In 1850 Francis Wayland, the president of Brown, framed the problem succinctly: "We have produced an article for which the demand is diminishing. We sell it at less than cost, and the deficiency is made up by charity. We give it away, and still the demand diminishes. Is it not time to inquire whether we cannot furnish an article for which the demand will be, at least, somewhat more remunerative?"[1] He was talking about the classical studies that still dominated the college curriculum—with a focus on classical languages, the medieval trivium, and religion. The emphasis was on tradition and piety rather than learning things that would prove useful in the modern world. "The single academy at West Point," he argued, "has done more toward the construction of railroads than all of our . . . colleges united."[2]

A MODERN CURRICULUM

After the Civil War, however, the college curriculum did begin to modernize and turn more practical, led by the example of the land-grant colleges, with their focus on engineering and agriculture and other forms of learning related to the practical work that graduates might pursue. The proportion of students seeking to enter the clergy, which had been the largest group in the student body early in the century, was declining, the proportion aiming for law and medicine was growing, and increasing numbers were going into business.[3] Student enrollments, after falling in the 1840s, began to rise in the 1850s and accelerated in the 1860s and 1870s. By 1869 there were 63,000 students in college, a number that rose to 116,000 in 1879, 157,000 in 1889, 238,000 in 1899, and 355,000 in 1909—an average increase of about 50 percent per decade.[4] With enrollments surging and the founding of colleges slowing, the average student body started to increase more rapidly: from only 47 in 1850, it rose to 131 in 1880, 157 in 1890, 243 in 1900, and 372 in 1910. This sharp growth in enrollments helped make marginal colleges more viable enterprises.

One reason for this change was the shift toward practical curriculum, which made college attendance seem more like a useful investment for a future career. Another reason was the rise of the elective system during the same period. Harvard kicked off the trend in 1869 by eliminating the old required curriculum and allowing students to choose from an array of courses in filling out their program of study. In the same year, Harvard also stopped combining conduct and scholarship in calculating student rank, choosing instead to grade students only by academic performance. The first of these changes made studies much more consumer friendly, which in turn made college attractive for a wider range of students. The second reinforced this consumer orientation by announcing that college was less about building character (how the college could shape you) than about acquiring useful cognitive skills (how the college could serve you). Both policies spread quickly throughout the system, initially to the larger public and private institutions that could afford to support the broader array of courses called for in the elective system and then, gradually, in attenuated form to the smaller schools.[5]

College leaders who made these changes did not necessarily do so for the explicit purpose of pleasing the educational consumer. People like Harvard's Charles W. Eliot framed the changes as a response to the growing specialization of knowledge in the emerging university and the need to abandon a narrow core of studies for all students. But intended or not, they did make college more attractive to a wider array of students, and other colleges felt compelled to adopt the changes in order to remain competitive in a tight educational market. These curriculum reforms seemed to address Wayland's complaint about the midcentury college model, but by themselves they did not deal with the other major problem facing the system, its weak academic reputation. In fact, eliminating program requirements could easily have signaled a decline in academic standards by making it easier for students to take courses that were more enjoyable but less intellectually rigorous. Electives meant that students, rather than the college, were setting the standards, potentially making the college more like a department store than a cathedral of learning.

ADDING A GRADUATE SCHOOL BUT KEEPING THE UNDERGRADS

The system in this period, however, responded to the credibility problem by importing elements of the German-model research university. Germany remade its large but lagging university system in the nineteenth century around the ideals of scientific research and advanced graduate education. It pioneered the PhD as the credential certifying research-based learning at the highest level and made this the entry ticket for a professorial position. American educators were entranced by this vision of the university and made regular pilgrimages to Germany to learn about the system and increasingly, by the 1870s and 1880s, to earn doctorates there. Johns Hopkins University, established in 1876, was the first American institution founded in line with this model, and Clark University (1887) was the second. Both represented a nearly pure case of adopting the German approach—remaining small, with a heavy focus on graduate education and research. This, however, was not the American norm. Most institutions that became research universities did so by adding a graduate school on top of a large and growing undergraduate program. By 1904 there were fifteen leading research universities in the United States: California (Berkeley), Chicago, Columbia, Cornell, Harvard, Hopkins, Illinois, Michigan, Minnesota, Massachusetts Institute of Technology (MIT), Pennsylvania, Princeton, Stanford, Wisconsin, and Yale—five small private universities, five comprehensive private universities, and five large public universities. These elite schools were also were the largest in the country, accounting in 1904 for 22 percent of all American college enrollments.[6]

Notice that Clark had already dropped off the list; therein lies a key part of our story. The problem was that the German model didn't translate very well to the U.S. context, and those who tried to copy it slavishly ran into trouble. Clark held the line on graduate education and had to struggle to survive on the modest enrollments and limited revenues that followed from this decision. Hopkins included undergraduate education only reluctantly, and several presidents tried to eliminate it, but competition eventually compelled them to preserve lower-level instruction. The American university, it turned out, couldn't flourish (or possibly even survive) without a strong array of undergraduate programs.

A large group of undergraduates served a variety of important functions for even the most research-oriented American universities. The research university was an enormously expensive proposition, which involved small class sizes and high faculty contact and which paid professors to carry out research. Major sources of federal research funding did not arise in American higher education until the Second World War (for now such funds came in modest amounts from private donations and foundations), so universities for the first half of the century had to generate internal sources to subsidize research.[7] A large pool of undergraduates brought a large amount of tuition money to support the whole enterprise. Even in public universities, where tuition was lower (and in a few cases nonexistent), undergraduates helped because state appropriations were in part allocated based on the number of enrolled students. Enrolling more undergrads justified hiring more professors, especially in the new era of the expanded elective curriculum, and large undergraduate classes required the hiring of graduate students as teaching assistants. Thus was born a central principle of the American university that has continued to the present day: cross-subsidy. In the U.S. model, each individual program of teaching and research in the institution does not have to support itself with its own dedicated revenue stream; instead, the university moves resources around internally to keep the various components afloat. The parts depend on the whole.

But the undergraduates in the new American research university did not just provide tuition and appropriations; they also became the primary base of donors for the university. Then as now, undergraduates were heading into more lucrative careers than the academics produced by doctoral programs. They became managers and professionals, earning more income and accumulating more wealth than the researchers turned out by the graduate school. These were the alumni who were going to contribute to the university's endowment and buy naming rights for new buildings on campus. Over the course of the nineteenth century, the American liberal arts college had become adept at tapping its graduates for the funds needed to support the enterprise, and this became particularly important when, at the end of the century, the enterprise added the expensive upper tier of graduate education.

Undergraduates also contributed one more crucial element to the American model of the research university: a broad base of political support. The German university could focus on abstruse research and advanced graduate study because of secure funding from the state. But a comparable aura of elitism was dangerous for American universities. In order to scrape off the old reputation for mediocrity they had accumulated earlier in the century, they needed to cloak themselves in the intellectual cachet of research and advanced learning. But they could not afford to be seen as remote from the public or disconnected from the practical life of the community. They needed to add the elite element to the higher ed package without abandoning either the populist or the practical. Heavily weighted toward undergraduates, the American research university that emerged at the start of the twentieth century assumed a lofty academic role while still retaining the feel and appeal of a people's college.

THE NEW SHAPE OF THE SYSTEM

By 1910, all of the core elements of the new research university were firmly in place. At the top was still a strong, entrepreneurial president appointed by a board of laymen, but now the makeup of the board of trustees had shifted away from clergymen to businessmen and professionals. At private institutions between 1860 and 1910, the proportion of clergy on the board fell from 39 to 17 percent while board members from business, law, and banking rose to 68 percent; only 9 percent were educators. At public institutions, the proportion of clergy on the board had never been high, and by 1910 businessmen had displaced lawyers as the largest occupational group; business, law, and banking accounted for 81 percent of the members; and only 7 percent were educators.[8]

New faculty hired at these institutions needed to have a PhD, and the recommendation for hiring them came from the faculty members of a new organizational unit within the university, the disciplinary department. The rise of the department was a sign of both the growing size of the institution and the growing emphasis on intellectual specialization. Only the experts in the field could judge the quality of faculty candidates and instructional programs, so the department took the lead in hiring and curriculum matters, which in turn decentralized power. These faculty were expected to engage in research, so a whole array of laboratories, specialized research journals, and professional organizations arose to support this effort. Pedagogy consisted of lectures for undergraduates and seminars for graduate students.

Another characteristic of the new university was the hegemonic position it assumed in American intellectual and professional life. It was not just an institution for acquiring certification in higher learning; it became the only credible place to get such certification. A major indicator of this was the role it suddenly assumed in the education of future professionals. Until the turn of the twentieth century, the primary route for entering the professions was apprenticeship. A student would work as an assistant to a doctor of lawyer for a while until deemed ready to enter practice. Prospective doctors and lawyers often attended college and some attended de facto medical or law schools, but most of the latter were freestanding enterprises independent of universities and had little pretension of academic rigor. But by 1910, the pressure was rising for professional education to join itself to the university. Only the latter had the scientific authority and educational standing to provide a strong launching pad for a professional career. Even less prestigious professions such as teaching felt the draw, as high-school-level normal schools began changing into teachers colleges, which later in the century evolved into regional state universities.

One last new element that the research university model contributed to the American system of higher education was hierarchy. The new structure introduced hierarchy in two related ways, both across the whole educational system and also within the domain of higher education. First, it created a clear ladder of educational attainment, each rung with its own institutional form. High schools fed into undergraduate colleges, and these in turn fed into graduate and professional schools. As a result of this change, high schools lost the ability to compete with colleges, but in return they won a position as the sole feeder institutions for colleges. Likewise, undergraduate programs fell below graduate schools in the newly stratified structure, but at the same time they gained a monopoly on providing access to graduate and professional study. Paralleling this structure was a hierarchy of academic credentials, from high school diploma to bachelor's degree to master's or professional degree to PhD.

A second emerging hierarchy ranked the various institutions of higher education in relation to each other. Previously, colleges had operated under conditions of formal equality. They were physically isolated and played to local markets, so there was little reason for them to interact with each other and little basis for establishing relative rank. But now a clear structure of stratification was becoming visible. At the top were research universities, with a monopoly on graduate education and preeminence in academic prestige and research production. Next were undergraduate colleges or universities, which offered bachelor's degrees; these included most public and private colleges and universities, including the land-grant schools. At the third tier came the teachers colleges, recently rising to college status. And the fourth tier consisted of a new entry into the game, the junior college, which offered the first two years of a four-year college experience, with the possibility of transfer to a four-year school or entry into a semiprofessional role.

So this was the structure of the system that emerged with the creation of the American research university at the start of the twentieth century. It built on the old nineteenth-century structure, but in the process it created a rationalized and stratified system that has persisted to the present day. It drew on the strengths of the old structure—adaptability, broad political and financial sources of support, and consumer orientation—while adding academic credibility and the promise of social and individual utility. This is the system that established the promise for what turned out to be a spectacular century of growth and rising accomplishment for American higher education.

But at this stage, in 1910, the system was more about promise than product. The elements were all there, the structure was in place, but the potential was far from being realized. This was particularly true at the research university. There were only fifteen or so out of 951 institutions of higher education that could claim to be taking on this role, and even for them, the research component was still quite marginal. There were only 9,000 graduate students in the United States, which amounted to a little more than 2 percent of the total number of college enrollments, and most of these were in science.[9] Undergraduates were hugely dominant within the system, even in the research universities. The scholarly productivity of faculty at the latter was modest, since research funds were short and research expertise still thin (most faculty still did not have the PhD). At other institutions of higher education, research was nonexistent. In many ways, it wasn't until the Second World War that university research really became a major-league enterprise. And that lag reinforces a central theme of this book—that the American system of higher education was good at building a structure and a capacity for accomplishment long before it was needed and there were means to capitalize on it.

In light of the limited extent of the system's actual commitment to graduate education and research, it is not surprising that some commentators found the new research university—and the system that it crowned—underwhelming in light of the German model. From the latter perspective, the Americans did everything wrong. They let undergraduates crowd out and undermine graduate education; they forced professors to teach too much, especially to undergrads; and what research they did was too focused on practical problems rather than research for its own sake as in the German vision. The most slashing critique came from Abraham Flexner, who had played an important role in helping to shape the new research university. In 1910 he wrote an extraordinarily influential study for the Carnegie Foundation for the Advancement of Teaching, which attacked the old model of the free-standing medical school and strongly endorsed incorporating medical education into the research university in order to give the profession a research base and university prestige. But in 1930, he wrote another book, which attacked the American university for having failed in its mission. His ideal was the German university and his American model was the old original Johns Hopkins, where he received his own PhD in 1884. Early on in the book, he outlines his case: "The great American universities which I shall discuss are composed of three parts: they are secondary schools and colleges for boys and girls; graduate and professional schools for advanced students; 'service' stations for the general public. The three parts are not distinct: the college is confused with the 'service' station and overlaps the graduate school; the graduate school is partly a college, partly a vocational school, and partly an institution of university grade."[10]

In his view, the only thing that made an institution "university grade" was the graduate school in pure form—where professors performed research and where they educated advanced graduate students who planned to become researchers themselves or members of the high professions. For him the undergraduate program that consumed so much of the faculty's effort was little more than a high school, which should be carried out elsewhere in order to avoid polluting the graduate enterprise. Among the professional schools, only medicine and law were deemed worthy of inclusion; schools of education and the like were nothing but vocational schools, which should be lodged elsewhere. In short, he mourned the distinctive path taken by the American system of higher education at the start of the century, which is the path that led the situation in the 1960s when the system started to look like a model for the world. Clark Kerr, who presided over the University of California during this heady decade, provides a pithy critique of Flexner's view: "The universities did all the wrong things—undergraduate instruction, professional schools (other than law and medicine), service activities, vocational courses, extension work. They did all the wrong things—and they entered their most Golden Age."[11]

Students Come to Embrace the College Experience

We have seen that the American system of higher education went through an evolution at the end of the nineteenth century. An academically undistinguished and radically overbuilt system needed credibility and needed students; by 1910 it had both. In the previous section, we saw how the research university brought academic recognition to a system that had long been a standing joke for European visitors, but it is less clear how adding a top layer to the system made college so much more attractive to students. One factor we saw that helped in the latter quest was that the colleges sought to make the curriculum more consumer friendly. By shifting from the traditional classical curriculum, with its strong emphasis on dead languages and religious piety, to a living-language curriculum that was more focused on skills useful in modern life, the system for the first time was able to make a case for the utility of attending college. High schools and land-grant colleges had both paved the way for these changes, and competition compelled the other parts of the system to follow suit. This was a start, but it still doesn't explain how middle-class families by the end of the century had so quickly come to see college attendance as an essential pursuit for their children.

The answer is that at this time a series of factors converged to turn college into the primary means by which middle-class families could pass on social position to the next generation. College had suddenly become the pipeline to a middle-class job. Below I explore how that happened, by examining the occupational and educational situation facing the middle class in this period. In the next section after the one following, I explore the other part of the equation: how employers came to prefer hiring college graduates.

The rise of the university model in the 1880s and the growing popularity of attending college coincided with a sharp increase in social pressure on the life chances of the college's traditional middle-class constituency. In the eighteenth and most of the nineteenth century in America, to be middle class was to be the owner of a small business. Wealthy people owned large businesses like a bank, trading firm, or plantation. The middling sort owned a farm or shop where they employed their family and a few workers. In town, this usually meant owning a small retail establishment or an artisanal production operation with its own attached store. It was a middle class of proprietors, and the entry point to this status was apprenticeship. A family would apprentice its son to a printer or shoemaker or shopkeeper, where he would live with the owner and learn the trade, move up to journeyman status while living and working in the shop, and with luck and some backing set up his own small business, eventually hiring his own apprentices and journeymen. In this situation, your social position was grounded in the business, and you passed on this position to your sons by having them take over this business.

The market revolution in the 1820s and 1830s in the United States began to disrupt this system. The rise of cheap transportation (canals and turnpikes) meant that the shops in town were no longer protected from competition from retailers and producers in other towns, even those in more distant cities. This competition forced producers to reduce costs and increase productive efficiency, and the result was a steady decline in both wages and prices across the whole nineteenth century. Under these circumstances, owners could no longer support a stable in-house workforce but needed to hire by the hour at the lowest rate and let people go when business was slack. Efficiencies of scale paid off, so enterprises grew larger. Increasingly, apprentices were just cheap, unskilled labor with no avenue for advancement, and proprietors were becoming large-scale businessmen. In short, the middle was disappearing.[12]

By the 1880s, the process had accelerated. The consolidation of businesses, combined with the emergence of steam power, increasingly transferred production to large-scale factories, and small retail shops were being squeezed out by the new large-scale department stores. The middle classes—if they hadn't already been pushed down into the working class or won a rare position as a large business owner—were finding themselves without a viable business to pass on to their children. The most promising possibilities for a middle-class life for the next generation were now in new forms of white-collar employment—in the corporations that were taking charge of a large manufacturing operations and in the emerging government bureaucracies.

THE CULTURE OF PROFESSIONALISM

The problem for these families was how to ensure that the white-collar workforce didn't just turn into a proletariat with a cleaner workplace. Here, college dropped to the stage as deus ex machina. The college degree became an insurance policy against proletarianization. Burton Bledstein explains the process at end of century in his compelling book, *The Culture of Professionalism: The Middle Class and the Development of Higher Education in America*. The idea is this: You don't want a job; you want a profession. Being a professional protects you from downward mobility and grants you autonomy and authority—an elevated status in a democratic society, made legitimate because it is grounded in specialized knowledge acquired through individual merit. And the institution that provides this knowledge and certifies this merit is the university. Bledstein puts it this way: "By and large the American university came into existence to serve and promote professional authority in society. More than in any other Western country in the last [nineteenth] century, the development of higher education in America made possible a social faith in merit, competence, discipline, and control that were basic to accepted conceptions of achievement and success."[13]

Professionalism burst on the American scene in 1880s. That decade alone saw the formation of no fewer than sixteen professional associations, ranging from chemists to political scientists, and saw massive increases in the number of professional students in universities (988 percent in dentistry, 142 percent in medicine, and 249 percent in law).[14] It turns out that in a market economy everyone praises competition but no one wants to experience it personally. Thus businesses construct corporations as a conspiracy against the market (to contain and control competition from other businesses as much as possible), and employees construct professions to accomplish the same goal in the workforce. But in a democracy, privileged exemption from the travails of the ordinary worker requires a strong justification. "Far more than other types of societies, democratic ones required persuasive symbols of the credibility of authority, symbols the majority of people could reliably believe just and warranted. It became the function of the schools in America to legitimize the authority of the middle class by appealing to the universality and objectivity of 'science.'"[15] With the emergence of the research university, science was now firmly located in higher education.

The culture of professionalism extended well beyond the bounds of the traditional high professions (law, medicine, clergy) to the new world of white-collar employment—to roles as managers in corporations, stores, and government bureaucracies. The ideal was to endow these positions with some of the same characteristics as the professions, such as autonomy, certified expertise, and meritocratic appointment. And having a degree from a college or university was the main element that linked these positions with the full-fledged professions and gave them credibility.

Another factor reinforced the central position played by higher education in this process of conferring middle-class standing. Elementary enrollments had been growing steadily in the United States since the first common schools appeared in the 1820s while high school enrollments remained quite low. Census data show that, by 1910, the average twenty-five-year-old American had eight years of schooling, which means that toward the end of the nineteenth-century elementary schools were filling up.[16] High school had been the protected do-main of middle-class families during most of the century, but in its last several decades, high school enrollments were beginning to expand to include a large number of working-class students. Under pressure from voters to increase access to educational opportunity, school districts began to build new high schools; as a result, high school enrollments increased sharply, doubling every decade from 1890 to the Second World War. For the high school's traditional middle-class constituency, this flood of newcomers threatened to dilute the for-mer exclusivity provided by high school credentials. Under these cir-cumstances, attending college looked increasingly attractive, since it had become the new zone of educational advantage, a way to mark yourself off from the common herd by assuming the mantle of the professional.[17]

THE GROWING LURE OF COLLEGE LIFE

So, with the upgraded status of the higher education system at the end of the century and with consumers' growing need for a college degree in order to get a good middle-class job, attending college became a useful pursuit for middle-class youth. At the same time, it also became a pleasurable pursuit. Recall the desperate straits facing the American college in 1880, when the ratio of colleges to population was at its historic peak. The number of institutions per million population rose from 5.2 in 1850 to 16.1 in 1880 and then declined to 9.8 in 1920.[18] So many sellers, so few buyers. Under these circumstances, a college's survival depended on its ability to draw more students in an extraor-dinarily competitive market. As we have seen, they helped make their product more consumer friendly by abandoning course requirements and shifting the curriculum toward more practical skills and knowl-edge. At the same time, they also sought to make college life more attractive—or, it is probably more accurate to say, they responded to student demands for these perks. The idea was that attending college would not only be a way to get a good job, but it would also be an enjoyable social experience—one that prospective students would eagerly anticipate, enrolled students would revel in, and alumni would remember fondly for years afterward. By the end of the century, this dream was realized; college had become a destination.

What came together suddenly on American college campuses in the last two decades of the nineteenth century was the full array of undergraduate extracurricular activities that characterize campus life today. Most centrally these included fraternities and sororities, which took charge of student social life; a wide variety of clubs and other campus organizations to engage students outside of classwork; and, of course, intercollegiate athletics. When students arrived on campus they found a large and complex array of student-run activities that operated independently of and often in conflict with the official academic regime of college studies. Entering this life was a process of immersion, which for most students became the defining experience of attending college.

At the heart of college life was football. The first intercollegiate football game was played between Princeton and Rutgers in 1869, but the sport didn't take off on campus until Walter Camp, a former player at Yale who become the sport's greatest promoter, revised the rules in the early 1880s to give it the familiar form it has today. From that point on, it spread with remarkable rapidity across college campuses, and the effort to organize intercollegiate play forced the isolated array of institutions to organize themselves into leagues. By 1915, 263 colleges were playing football against each other.[19] The game became a center of student social life. Sports had existed on a small scale on college campuses in the mid-nineteenth century, but the focus then was on competition between classes within the college, such as juniors against seniors. But now the focus was on the effort to defeat rival colleges on the football field, which led students and alumni to develop a close identification with their home institution by rallying behind the home team. With football came such now familiar collegiate elements as letter sweaters, fight songs, cheerleaders, alma maters, homecoming, and the tradition of wearing your school colors with pride and defiance.

Another consequence of the rise of football was that the college— after years of obscurity—became part of the larger popular culture.

Athletic contests became major news on sports pages and they helped burnish the populist image of an institution that could otherwise have easily been seen as archly elitist. Partly because of this newly accessible component of college life and partly because college was now becoming a central part of the middle-class American experience, college life started to become the subject of magazine articles and the setting for popular novels. For college administrators, this change was a bonanza of positive public relations. They now found themselves running an institution that had both academic credibility and popular appeal, that was able to offer students a way both to get a good job and have a good time. The scrappy but disreputable higher education system of the nineteenth century had now emerged as a popular and prestigious institution deeply integrated into middle-class American life.

Employers Come to Value the College Graduate

We can understand why middle-class students were now choosing to attend college in large numbers, since doing so was both economically useful and socially enjoyable. But that doesn't explain why employers were now willing to hire them. For most of the nineteenth century, employers had in fact disdained college men, arguing that the college experience disqualified them for hard work. Andrew Carnegie was one of the leading critics: "In my own experience I can say that I have known few young men intended for business who were not injured by a collegiate education. Had they gone into active work during the years spent at college they would have been better educated men in every true sense of that term. The fire and energy have been stamped out of them, and how to so manage as to live a life of idleness and not a life of usefulness, has become the chief question with them."[20] However, by the early twentieth century, Carnegie and other corporate leaders had become major supporters of colleges and came to prefer hiring college graduates in management positions. What happened?

As David Brown has explained, toward the end of the century these leaders came to realize that the college man could be the answer to a major organizational problem that they had to confront.[21] This was the period when the corporation arose as the organizational form for controlling major business enterprises. What happens in a corporation is that the personal control of the owner becomes diffused and rationalized into a bureaucratic structure of administration. People like Carnegie now had to rely on a large number of managerial employees to take care of the wide range of activities of the corporation in a manner that was both competent and in line with corporate priorities. It was not easy to figure out which potential hires would be able to meet both criteria. In a small firm, the newcomer could start on the factory floor and work his way up the ladder, demonstrating his skill and loyalty along the way. But this was not a practical model for a giant corporation that needs to hire hundreds of managers to fill its administrative needs.

Brown argues that the college experience provided both elements required of the good manager. The skills required for bureaucratic work were not narrowly technical, in the sense of requiring specific knowledge about how to forge steel. These employees were not going to be metallurgists or engineers but managers. They needed to have a general ability to deploy the verbal and cognitive skills required to function within the setting of a complex organization. The new college environment at the end of the century was just such a social setting. They also needed to be comfortable assuming positions of authority. Again, being a college man meant that you were being socialized in a group of middle-class peers who saw management and professional life as their natural destiny. And your experience in college life helped prepare you in the interpersonal skills and leadership roles you will assume later on the job. In addition, corporations also needed to hire managers who were trustworthy and were aligned with the norms of the larger organization. So why not hire college men, who have been socialized in the norms of college life and pledged their loyalty to the college community?

As Brown notes, these are qualities that arise from the college experience but not necessarily from the formal academic curriculum. Ethan Ris develops this point further, arguing that it was explicitly the new extracurriculum at the end-of-century American college that provided future managers with the skills and loyalty they would need on the job.[22] He sees three skills in particular that students acquired at college and that were and are salient to management work. One is autonomous productivity. Students were given broad assignments to complete and then allowed a lot of space and time to work things out on their own, seeking help as needed but not receiving close supervision. Just like bureaucratic work. Another is hierarchical proficiency. Students needed to learn how to function in the complex and often opaque structure of the university. This was and is a system with multiple hierarchies—freshman to senior; assistant to full professor; faculty, chair, dean, provost, president—where the organizational chart is not much help in figuring out how to get things done and where you need to learn how to read the structure correctly and approach the right person. It's also a place where students develop their own roles, moving through a student hierarchy to positions like team captain, head cheer leader, fraternity president, and club organizer. A bureaucracy has many of the same elements, which employees need to negotiate effectively. A third skill is institutional loyalty. One of the things that the new university was good at was socializing students to identify with the institution and the team and the fraternity. These graduates have worn the colors, supported the team, and donated to the endowment—exactly the kind of team players needed on the job.

John Thelin notes that "a popular banner found in student dormitory rooms in the 1890s proclaimed, 'Don't Let Your Studies Interfere with Your Education!'"[23] The point, of course, is that the student culture in the period was in opposition to academic learning, which it certainly was. A mound of evidence attests to the student desire to do the minimum required to pass classes without unduly intruding on the quality of social life. But it may be that we should take the banner's admonition seriously. Maybe it was indeed the student-run extracurriculum at the early twentieth-century university that provided the core knowledge and skill that students would need in their future roles as corporate employees.

The larger story is that the American system of higher education

maintained its consumer orientation even as it was enjoying the benefits that came from its new association with scientific research and
advanced learning. Adding a graduate school to the university didn't
do anything to diminish the hold that undergraduate programs had
on the institution. If anything, the move toward high-level research
made the institution even more dependent on the financial support,
political legitimacy, and practical impact that came from the undergraduates, whose desire for a good job and a good time had to be
honored. In order to become an academic powerhouse, the university
also had to become a party school.

4

MUTUAL SUBVERSION

The Liberal and the Professional

As we have seen, the American system of higher education thrives on contradiction. It not only refuses to resolve its contradictions one way or the other but also embraces the tensions that arise from working at cross purposes. It resolutely maintains itself as an institutional arena that is elite and populist and practical all at the same time and often even on the same campus. As a result it has come in for a lot of criticism. In 1930, Abraham Flexner called for the university to abandon everything except graduate education.[1] But instead, the system doubled down on the mixed model, and thirty years later moved on to fame and fortune. Today, critics are telling the system to disaggregate the muddled mix of functions into their component parts—undergraduate instruction here, research there, professional preparation somewhere else—and to get rid of all the expensive extras, such as food courts and rock-climbing walls and football. To their great frustration, the system declines to do so.

In the next four chapters, I examine four central tensions that run through the system—between the liberal and the professional, between access and advantage, between college as a public good and college as a private good, and between the public college and the private college. In doing so I'm shifting from the largely chronological account in chapters 2 and 3 to a structural analysis of contradictory impulses and functions that animate the system, using historical developments in the twentieth century as the material for exploring those contradictions.

In this chapter I examine two alternative motifs in the history of the American system of higher education during the last century. The dominant motif is that over the years professional education has become dominant in colleges and universities, in the process subverting the earlier function of providing liberal education. The more muted contrapuntal motif is that, over the same period of time, liberal education has gradually pushed back against professional education, in the process quietly subverting it. My aim is to show how these two motifs weave together into a fugue of mutual subversion, in which the professional has come to dominate the goals of higher education while the liberal has come to dominate its content.

Point: The Shift from the Liberal to the Professional

One recurring theme in the history of American higher education is that the professional has been displacing the liberal. In a book from a decade ago, Norton Grubb and Marvin Lazerson develop this theme with great effectiveness, arguing that American education, especially at the tertiary level, has become increasingly vocationalized and professionalized over the years.[2] At the root of this change is what they call "the education gospel," the firmly held belief that education exists in order to provide society with the job skills it needs and to provide individuals with the job opportunities they want. The authors acknowledge that this belief has yielded some real social and educational benefits. It has made higher education more attractive both to students seeking jobs and to employers seeking workers, and it has provided a strong basis for public support of higher education by demonstrating that the university is not simply a stronghold protecting the privileges of the elite but a people's college promoting the public welfare. In this sense, it helps support the idea of college as a public good, an issue we'll explore in chapter 5. But they also point out the downside of this shift toward the professional. From that angle, the change has replaced broad liberal curriculum with a narrower vocational curriculum, undercut the quality of learning by focusing on winning jobs rather than gaining knowledge, and stratified educational programs and institutions according to the status of students' future occupations.

What's new about Grubb and Lazerson's book is their view that this trend toward the vocational has a plus side, whereas the literature in general portrays the change as overwhelmingly negative. But the argument that this change has been taking place is a commonplace in the historical scholarship on American higher education. In Laurence Veysey's classic account, the rise of the American university in the late nineteenth century was characterized by the emergence of utility and research as dominant orientations, only partially offset by a lingering attachment to liberal culture.[3] As we have seen, Clark Kerr argues that the American university drew on two European precursors—the English college, with its emphasis on undergraduate liberal education, and the German graduate school, with its emphasis on research and graduate education—but then added a third distinctively American element, the land-grant college, with its emphasis on vocational education and providing practical solutions to public problems.[4]

Most historical accounts have emphasized this third element, which, in combination with the second, is seen as pushing the university from a focus on providing students with a liberal education to a focus on preparing them for work. The evidence in support of this position is strong. The United States did not invent the university, but it did invent three distinctive forms of higher education, all of which had a strong vocational mission. The land-grant college was designed to prepare graduates in the practical arts and to enhance industry. The normal school was established solely to prepare teachers for a rapidly expanding public school system. And the junior college and its heir, the community college, were invented primarily to provide vocational education for what some founders called the "semi-professions."[5] The large majority of college students in the United States today are enrolled in colleges and universities that have their origins in one of these three types of vocational institutions.

The main explanation for the growing vocational orientation of the

American university is that it has just been responding to consumer demand. As we saw in chapter 2, in the absence of strong state funding and state control, institutions of higher education in the United States have always been subject to strong market pressures. They depend heavily on student enrollments to generate income, in the form of both student-paid tuition and per capita state appropriations, which means they have to cater to the demands of the consumer. They also rely on income from alumni donors and (by the mid-twentieth century) research grants. Their partial autonomy from state control gives them the freedom to maneuver effectively in the educational market in order to adapt to changing consumer preferences, donor demands, and research opportunities. Over the years, student consumers have increasingly expressed a preference for getting a good job over getting a liberal education, and donors and research funding agencies have demonstrated their own preferences for useful education and usable knowledge.

As we saw in chapter 3, the decline in viability of small businesses in the late nineteenth century threw middle-class families into the arms of the university. No longer able to will to their heirs the family shop, they turned to higher education for an alternative way to transmit social position to their children. The college experience provided the skills and values needed in the new professionalized form of white-collar work, and the college diploma certified that the holder's entry into management was the result not of privilege but of individual merit. Under this new vocational rationale for going to college, getting a liberal education would seem beside the point.

The newfound utility of going to college spurred a massive growth in enrollments. In the first three decades of the twentieth century, the population of the United States grew by 75 percent and college enrollment grew by 400 percent.[6] By 1924, 10 percent of young people were in college.[7] By 1930, the United States, with three times the population of the United Kingdom, had twenty times the number of college students.[8] Business and engineering were now the two dominant areas of study for undergraduates, and nearly two-thirds of students were there to prepare for a particular occupation or profession.[9] Academic leaders such as Robert M. Hutchins, Abraham Flexner, and Thorstein Veblen all railed against the rise of professional-practical education and the growing role of business, which they saw as polluting the academic purity of higher education and its reputation for excellence. But this had little effect on students, whose aspirations were practical rather than liberal.[10]

Throughout the twentieth century, the prime centers of growing enrollments were the new broad-access institutions emerging at the lower levels of the system, where the primary focus was on preparing students for the middle-class workforce: junior (and later, community) colleges, urban commuter colleges, and the teachers colleges that were evolving into regional state universities. The process kept accelerating toward the end of the century. Steven Brint's analysis shows that, between 1970 and 2000, "a period in which the system grew by 50 percent, almost every field which constituted the old arts and sciences core of the undergraduate college was in absolute decline. This includes not only all of the humanities and social sciences (except psychology and economics) but also the physical sciences and mathematics."[11]

Counterpoint: The Pushback of the Liberal against the Professional

The evidence is strong in support of the thesis that American higher education has long seen the expansion of the professional at the expense of the liberal. However, in many ways this argument may misrepresent what has really been going on. Instead of professionalizing liberal education, maybe we've really been liberalizing professional education.

There is also a lot of historical evidence to support this counter thesis—especially when you look at the *curriculum content* of the expanding professional sector of higher education. Although most of the growth in higher education has been in the professional schools rather than in the core disciplinary departments, Brint points out that the curriculum of the professional schools has become increasingly disciplinary. As he puts it: "Occupational and professional programs have moved closer to the center of academic life partly because they have modeled themselves on the arts and sciences—developing similarly abstract vocabularies, similarly illuminating theoretical perspectives, and similarly rigorous conceptual schemes."[12]

Professional education has only recently taken this academic turn. Before the twentieth century, most professional training took place by means of apprenticeship to an experienced practitioner, with the academic component of this preparation largely consisting of reading the books in the practitioner's library.[13] The shift toward the academic occurred as a result of the gradual incorporation of professional education into the university beginning in the late nineteenth century. And since the Second World War, the academic content of professional education in a wide range of fields has steadily increased, only recently provoking a reaction demanding more attention to practice-based preparation.

Consider how academic the content of professional education has become in most professional schools, starting with the two most extreme cases, divinity and law. Practicing clergy have long derided their seminary training as largely useless in developing the skills they need to practice their profession effectively. Divinity schools are notorious for focusing primarily on the academic study of theology, not on preaching, pastoral care, finance, leadership, and the other central practices in the profession.[14] Likewise law schools (especially at elite universities) have long focused on the study of jurisprudence, logic, and argumentation, all central elements in a liberal education. Little time is spent on developing skills at doing things that form the core of professional legal practice, like writing briefs, arguing cases in court, negotiating contracts, and handling clients.[15] Although in recent years both fields have developed movements to introduce clinical professional studies within the almost entirely academic programs in their fields, these efforts have encountered considerable resistance.

But what about other professional fields, which have reputations for being less academic? Teacher education, for example, is considered a baldly vocational program by the arts and sciences faculty on campus. But the graduates of these programs have long complained that their professional education is relentlessly theoretical—focused on the psychology of learning and curriculum, the sociology of the teacher and the school, and the history and philosophy of education, while offering little guidance about how to carry out the role of classroom teacher—that is, teaching a curriculum to a particular group of students.[16] Business schools have the same reputation. The master's in business administration (MBA) in most business schools is remarkably abstract and academic, largely cut off from practices in the real world of business. Whereas the dominant discipline in education schools is psychology, the dominant discipline in business schools is economics. An MBA provides a grounding in the theories of economics, enhanced by studies in the sociology of organizations, the psychology of effective leadership, and other disciplinary explorations of the business environment; business practice is something students are expected to learn on the job. Business education used to be more practical in orientation, but reforms initiated by the Ford Foundation and Carnegie Corporation in the 1950s promoted a graduate-level model that was academic, research-based, and disciplinary.[17] Medical education has a much stronger component of preparation for clinical practice than most other professional programs, but even here most clinical training takes place after completion of the four-year medical degree program, which is dominated by academic study of the human sciences.

If the content of professional education has been growing more academic, then how can we understand the growth of professional schools relative to the arts and sciences? The traditional interpretation of the latter development is that the disciplines have been losing out to the professions within the university, thus demonstrating the growing triumph of the vocational over the liberal. Instead, however, the growth of professional schools may be a sign of the expanding power of the disciplines. Maybe the university is not becoming more professional, but professional schools are becoming more academic. From this view, the theoretical is actually displacing the practical in higher education. The disciplines are in effect colonizing the professional schools, transforming professional education into liberal education in professional garb. Steven Brint's analysis of American faculty members in 1992 shows that 12.4 percent of professors with degrees in the natural sciences were teaching in professional schools (net of people moving the other direction), along with 8.8 percent of those with social science degrees and 6.5 percent of those with humanities degrees.[18]

My own field in the history of education is an interesting case in point. Only about a third of the members of the American History of Education Society are located in history departments, whereas two-thirds are in schools of education. One interpretation is that this represents a decline in the field, showing a loss of our identity as historians and the subordination of the discipline to the professional mission of the education school. But the interpretation I favor is the reverse: that we are expanding history's influence into the realm of professional education. With the gradual shrinking of history departments, professional schools such as in education have provided the opportunity for historians to address a wider audience. I've been teaching in education schools for thirty years, and my job is to provide students with a liberal education. I teach critical reading and analytical writing, and the material I use for this is history. In many ways, students in professional schools need historians more than do students in history departments. Unlike the latter, education students are not in college to get a liberal education, but being there offers us an opportunity to give them a liberal education anyway. In this way, the growth of professional education in the university provides rich opportunities for the growth of the disciplines. The latter is unintended, even unwanted, but it is nonetheless real.

From this perspective, then, the shift toward the professional and the vocational in the history of American higher education has been more rhetorical than substantive.[19] Maybe it is best understood as largely a marketing tool, which makes a university education seem more useful and relevant than it really is. Levine shows how liberal arts colleges after World War I started marketing their traditional liberal programs as places to learn the practical skills needed for success in the white-collar workplace.[20] We see colleges and universities doing the same today. They emphasize the usefulness of liberal learning—as training in business-relevant skills in communications, problem solving, critical thinking, and entrepreneurship. Over the past century, higher education in general may have simply been relabeling old disciplinary studies as new professional programs—more spin than substance. This is an old story in higher education, where the medieval curriculum and medieval structure of degrees have persisted in the face of enormous changes in economy and society in the last thousand years.

If the disciplines have indeed subverted the professional schools in higher education, one explanation is academic inertia. Old curriculum content keeps colonizing new institutional forms and gaining new rationales for its relevance: a case of old wine in new bottles. Another explanation comes from Ralph Turner's characterization of American education as a system of contest mobility.[21] From this perspective, the aim of education is to prepare students to compete effectively in the contest for social positions, and that means a system that maintains maximum flexibility for students by providing an education that allows access to the broadest array of occupational possibilities. In practical terms, this leads us to defer specialization until the last possible moment in order to keep our options open. Thus American education emphasizes general education over specialized education, and this is true even in the most advanced studies and in professional training programs. So, unlike most of the rest of the world, doctoral programs in the United States require extensive coursework before launching students into a dissertation, and most of these courses are aimed at providing a general background in the field. At the same time, professional programs of study include a hefty component of liberal arts content. Both PhD students and MBA students want to be prepared for a variety of possible positions and not just one, and our consumer-responsive system of higher education gladly accommodates them.

Trying to Resolve the Paradox

So we have two opposing theses about the history of American higher education. One says that this has been a story of growing market influence, which has elevated professional education over liberal education. The other says that this is a story of curriculum inertia and consumer ambition, in which liberal education has perpetuated itself by colonizing professional education and general education has displaced specialized education. Both arguments have a lot of evidence to support them, and I don't want to abandon either. But how can we resolve these differences? I argue that these two themes can be brought together in harmony if we understand how they both resonate with several fundamental characteristics of American higher education. One such characteristic is *stratification*: the peculiar dynamic that organizes American education into an extended hierarchy. The other is *formalism*: the peculiar dynamic in American education that creates a gap between form and substance, between the purpose of education and its content.

POSITION IN THE EDUCATIONAL PECKING ORDER

As we have seen, stratification is at the heart of American education. It's the price we pay for the system's broad accessibility. We let everyone in, but they all get a different experience, and they all win different social benefits from these experiences. In this way the system is both strongly populist and strongly elitist, allowing ordinary people a high possibility of getting ahead through education and a low probability of getting ahead very far. We will explore this issue more fully in the next chapter.

If stratification is a central component in elementary and secondary education, it is the dominant element in higher education. In this way, as in others, American universities are American schools on steroids. A college or university's position in the academic pecking order is a fact of life that shapes everything else in that institution. And one of the key ways that institutions differ according to academic rank is in their location on the spectrum between the vocational and the liberal. At the bottom of the hierarchy are community colleges, which have a strong identity as places that provide practical vocational preparation for a wide variety of occupational positions. At the top are the leading research universities, which have an equally strong identity as places that provide theoretical and liberal education, even in programs designed to prepare professionals. In between is an array of colleges and universities that are more practical than the schools at the top and more liberal than the schools at the bottom. In the public sector of higher education in my own state of California, the community college system is at the bottom, the University of California system is at the top, and the California State University system (mostly former teachers colleges) is in the middle. Every state has its own equivalent distribution. It's just the way things are.

What this system of stratification suggests is that the changing historical balance between the liberal and professional, like so much else about American higher education, has varied according to the institution's position on the status ladder. So the expansion of community colleges and regional state universities have represented a shift toward the vocational, while the liberal disciplines have been holding their own at research universities and even expanding into professional programs. That is what observers like Brint, Richard Chait, and Andrew Abbott have concluded.[22] If so, then what we're observing is just a simple bifurcation of change processes, where the professional is subverting the liberal at the bottom of the system while the liberal is subverting the professional at the top. From this perspective, the resulting dualism is just another case of stratified access to knowledge, which is an old story in American education at all levels.

THE RHYTHMIC DEVELOPMENT OF THE SYSTEM: VOCATIONALIZE, LIBERALIZE, REPEAT

This characterization is true, as far as it goes. But I suggest that what's really going on is both more complicated and more interesting than this. There is a fascinating double dynamic that runs through the history of American higher education, pushing the system simultaneously to become both more professional and more liberal. Like so much else about the system, this process has operated through market mechanisms rather than conscious planning. It's a story of how individual institutions have struggled to establish and enhance their positions in the intensely competitive higher education market. The result is a set of institutional trajectories that are rational from the perspective of each institution's interests. But these trajectories accumulate into a dynamic structure of higher education that is both a bit pathological (in the way it's at odds with itself) and a bit dysfunctional (in its social impact).

The general pattern is this: the system expands by adding a new lower tier of institutions that are more vocational in orientation than those already in existence. Over time these new institutions zealously imitate their higher status predecessors by shifting toward producing a more liberal form of education. Then another tier of institutions comes forward to fill the vacated vocational role. Thus the system as a whole is continually expanding the realm of vocational education while individual institutions are relentlessly turning away from the vocational and aspiring to the liberal.

As I noted in chapter 1, there are three core dynamics that fuel these processes. One is that existing institutions of higher education enjoy enormous advantages over newcomers: they have more social capital (since they have educated society's leaders), more cultural capital (since they have already enlisted the best academic talent), and more economic capital (since they have established access to wealthy alumni and accumulated substantial endowments). And given this huge advantage, newly established institutions have had trouble competing with their predecessors on academic prestige, so they have instead tended to offer to serve useful social roles that the earlier ones did not, like preparing engineers and teachers—that is, they tended to be less liberal and more vocational.[23]

The second core dynamic is that institutions at all levels of the status order in higher education have a strong incentive to seek a higher level. Moving up promises to increase an institution's enrollments, grants, contributions, faculty recruitment, public influence, and overall prestige. The beneficiaries of upward mobility include everyone associated with the institution. Administrators enjoy credit for accomplishing the rise in rank, earn higher salaries and greater national prestige, find themselves quoted more frequently in the media, and find donors more willing to contribute, students more willing to apply, and faculty more willing to accept an offer of employment. For faculty, having a better letterhead provides more access to positions of leadership in professional organizations, journals, and government panels; increases their likelihood of winning research grants and professional awards; makes journals and book publishers more open to publishing their work; wins them more speaking and visiting scholar invitations; and earns them higher pay. Students, in turn, enjoy the glow of association with an institution higher up the pecking order, as embodied in the question that college-age students ask when encountering each other: "Where do you go to school?" This is a major reason why students are so eager to wear their school logo, which serves as major status marker. The biggest benefit, however, is the payoff that higher institutional standing brings to students in the job market, an issue I will explore in greater depth in the next chapter. Students even gain when their college climbs the status ladder after they have graduated, since they then enjoy association with an institution is more distinguished than the one they attended, one that today might not even admit them.

In order to move up the ladder, institutions need to imitate their betters, adopting the educational forms and functions that worked so well for those above them. Of course, since the older schools have a huge advantage in the status race, odds are that the aspirations of the newcomers will not be met. But this doesn't eliminate continuing hopes for future glory. As is true with the aspirations that individual citizens harbor for personal social mobility, the successes of the few are enough to keep hope alive for the many. High possibilities can trump low probabilities in the mind of the aspirant. Every up-and-coming college president looks at the great historical success stories of institutional mobility for their inspiration: Berkeley, Hopkins, Chicago, and Stanford were all relative latecomers who made it to the top. We could be next.

The third dynamic in the system is that expansion comes by introducing new institutions rather than by expanding the old ones. Existing colleges have every reason for letting others handle the influx. To increase enrollments would be to dilute the college's social exclusiveness, its academic reputation, and its distinctive identity. They don't want to alienate their constituency by going downscale toward vocationalism. Better to segment the market by holding the high ground for yourself and letting newcomers establish positions in the less valuable ground below you. That way, the system grows by maintaining the classic dual principles of American education—accessibility and exclusivity.

Let's look at how this process has played out over time. In the beginning, there were the colonial colleges. Through the luck of being first more than through intellectual eminence, these colleges established a dominant position that proved largely unshakable over the next two centuries. Included in their number were those schools that much later labeled themselves the Ivy League, such as Harvard, Yale, Princeton, Columbia, and Penn. They were followed in the nineteenth century by a series of public colleges that eventually developed into the flagship state universities. Most of the first group and many of the second came together to form what is now the top tier of American higher education: elite research universities. The institutions in this tier are the most prestigious, selective, and academically credible in the country; they have the greatest wealth, offer the most liberal curriculum, and educate the smallest proportion of students.

Next up was an American invention, the land-grant college. These institutions were funded by an array of public land distributions, starting in the 1830s and continuing through the end of the century (most particularly the Morrill Acts of 1862 and 1890). They were explicitly (though not exclusively) given a vocational mission. In the words of the original Morrill Act, these colleges were intended "to teach such branches of learning as are related to agriculture and the mechanic arts . . . in order to promote the liberal and practical education of the industrial classes in the several pursuits and professions of life."[24] These institutions became the core of the second tier of American higher education, made up of public universities below the top level, often identified by the label "A&M" or the word "state" in the title, to distinguish them from the flagship state university.[25]

The next arrival was another invention, the normal school, which began before the Civil War and flourished in the second half of the nineteenth century. These schools were founded for explicitly vocational purposes, to train schoolteachers. They formed the core of what evolved into the third tier of American higher education, the regional state universities that educate the lion's share of university students in the country.[26]

Last up was the junior college, which first emerged in the 1920s and later evolved into the community college. This became the fourth and final tier in the system. Like the land-grant college and the normal school, its official mission was vocational, in this case to prepare people for semiprofessional job roles (i.e., jobs below the level sought by graduates of four-year colleges).

These are the four tiers of American higher education. As you go down the hierarchy, these institutions progressively show the following characteristics. They have arisen more recently, adopted a more vocational mission, opened themselves to a broader range of students, and channeled graduates to lower-level occupations. And each of the lower three tiers continues to show more vocational tendencies than the tier above it.

However—and this is the crucial point—these institutions all tried very hard to run away from their original vocational mission in order to imitate the high-status liberal model offered by the top tier. The result, of course, was not a replication of the latter model so much as a pale imitation. For each tier as a whole and for most of the institutions within it, attaining the next level up the scale was simply not possible. The incumbents retained too many advantages, and the newcomers did not have any of the three forms of institutional capital (social, cultural, or economic) in sufficient quantities to compete effectively with their betters. But this did not keep them from trying.

The pattern over time is clear. Students wanted the most socially advantageous form of college education they could get, and this meant one that looked as much as possible like the Ivies and that opened up the maximum number of job opportunities. So, under pressure from consumers, each new tier of institutions expanded liberal studies at the expense of more narrowly focused vocational training. As the research university became the hegemonic model for American higher education in the early twentieth century, most of the institutions in the second and third tiers evolved into places that called themselves, and looked like, universities. Land-grant colleges led the way in this development. Normal schools had farther to go and their evolution took longer, but they got there as well. Starting as the equivalent of high schools in the mid-nineteenth century, they evolved into teacher colleges at the turn of the twentieth century, became state liberal arts colleges in the 1930s and 1940s, and finally turned into full-service state universities in the 1950s–70s.

The exception in this evolutionary process was the community college, but it wasn't for lack of trying. Large numbers of students in junior colleges and community colleges have long been voting with their feet for transfer programs that allow them access to liberal education at four-year colleges and universities.[27] For these students, the community college's main function is to provide the first two years of the liberal education curriculum they will need at the next level.[28] If past practice had persisted, this consumer pressure would have forced these institutions to develop into universities, just like their predecessors in land-grant colleges and normal schools. But during the twentieth century, states generally refused to allow junior colleges to grant four-year degrees. Instead, they were encouraged to develop into the enormous community college system we see today. In recent years, some cracks are appearing in the wall barring upward mobility for these institutions, as Florida, California, Ohio, and other states are beginning to permit them to offer BA programs in selected fields.

PUBLIC GOOD, PRIVATE GOOD

The case of the community college raises an important issue about the historical pattern I've been describing—where the system continually expands by opening new vocationally oriented institutions, which then gradually evolve back toward the liberal mean. If consumers were consistent in demanding access to a liberal education (in order to provide the widest array of social opportunities), why were all of the expansion colleges explicitly vocational? Why not just open new liberal arts colleges that were more accessible to the public?

The answer lies in the tension between college as a private good and college as a public good. College is a private good to the extent that its benefits accrue primarily to the individuals who receive the education and own the resulting diploma. College is a public good to the extent that its benefits go to the population as a whole, including both people who do and do not attend college. As we saw in chapter 2, the distinctiveness of the American system of higher education was that it emerged in a time when colleges did not have reliable state support. Instead of being created by the state for the benefit of all, they arose as private nonprofit institutions designed to meet the needs of local landowners and religious sects. As a result, they needed to attract and retain tuition-paying student-consumers in order to sustain themselves financially. The American college in the early- to mid-nineteenth century functioned as a private good, with primary benefits going to its founders and graduates but not necessarily to the larger community. From these roots arose the system's strong orientation toward serving the needs of consumers.

By the second half of the nineteenth century, however, the activity in founding colleges shifted strongly toward the public sector. State governments were the ones who created the state universities, land-grant colleges, and normal schools that constituted the arenas of growth for the higher education system. By the early twentieth century, the large majority of college foundings and nearly all of the growth in college enrollments occurred in the public domain.[29] As we saw, these institutions retained some private elements, since founding continued to provide benefits to locals and since they needed student tuition in order to stay afloat. But nonetheless, they were established by the state, controlled by the state, and largely funded by the state. This was not the same as granting a charter to Middlebury College and then leaving it on its own. The new colleges were state enterprises, which meant that lawmakers had to justify supporting them in light of how they served state interests. In the zero-sum game of state finances, money that went to public colleges came at the expense of other public priorities, such as elementary and secondary education, infrastructure, and public safety.

Consumers' interest in higher education is social mobility. College allows them to get a good job and lead a good life, by enabling them to move up socially from their current family position or to preserve the advantage their family already enjoys. Governments can and often do choose to view promoting social mobility as a public good, since it has the potential to promote social equity and it helps preserve social order by enhancing the legitimacy of the state. And lawmakers need to be responsive to consumer demand for college access simply because consumers are also voters. It's difficult for any democratic government to deny wide public access to an attractive public institution such as a university. But states have to balance this demand for educational access against other priorities for the public purse. And this is particularly the case for the demand for mobility via higher ed, where it is undeniable that the primary benefits go to the students whose life chances are improved by a college degree. For lawmakers, then, it comes down to a question of how much they are willing to use public funds to subsidize private ambition.

Everyone is required to attend elementary and secondary schools, so public funding clearly makes sense in this case. But college attendance is voluntary and large numbers of high school graduates never go on to the next level. Today, 34 percent do not attend college; in 1900 the proportion was 98 percent.[30] So this raises important questions, such as why should we tax everyone to send other people's children to college? And what public benefit justifies state investment in higher education?

If the private interest in higher education is in promoting social mobility, the public interest is in promoting social efficiency. Universities provide society with the productive skills it needs in order to support economic growth and enhance the general welfare. It's an investment in human capital that will pay benefits for the entire population. In addition, universities produce research that helps deal with pressing social and economic problems and that supports national power. For these reasons, it made perfect sense for governments in the later nineteenth century to use state appropriations and federal land grants to support the expansion of higher education. And it made sense in particular for them to target the forms of higher education that promised to provide practical, vocational education. These are the kinds of institutions most focused on promoting social efficiency through human capital production and thus serve the public good.

This continuing state interest in promoting social efficiency, when combined with the continuing consumer interest in social mobility, is what produced the seesaw pattern of historical evolution that I have been detailing in this chapter. States kept introducing new vocational forms of higher education and consumers kept diverting them toward the liberal education model they preferred, which offered the widest array of social opportunities. This is what happened with land-grant colleges and normal schools.[31] When it came to the third iteration of this dynamic, with the introduction of junior and community colleges in the twentieth century, states started dragging their feet—and for good reason.

The problem was that each time in the past when states had permitted the liberalization of vocational colleges, the cost shot up dramatically. It is much more expensive to provide a liberal education in the full array of college subjects than it is to provide a vocational education in a few specialized domains—engineering and agriculture, in the case of land-grant colleges, and teaching, in the case of normal schools. In addition, consumers did not stop with the demand for access to liberal education. They extended these demands to include access to the full array of graduate educational opportunities offered by the institution that came to crown the system of higher education at the start of the twentieth century, the full-service university. First land-grant colleges and then normal schools evolved into liberal arts colleges and later into universities with a full array of graduate schools. This evolution provided an extraordinary increase in access to higher education for American students, well ahead of the rest of the world. But it came at an enormous cost. One consequence of this was that legislators became wary of subsidizing the evolution of the latest entry into the higher education system, the community colleges, into universities. Another consequence, as we will see in chapter 7, was the rise of a taxpayer revolt in the latter part of the twentieth century, which started putting fiscal constraints on the ability of states to keep fueling the expansion of higher ed.

So far the community college has largely been blocked from pursuing the path of its predecessors. However, as I noted earlier, student consumers in large numbers have been dodging vocational programs and opting to take liberal arts courses with the hope of transferring to a university. But is the upward mobility process still going on for institutions in the second and third tiers of the system? I think so. Many of the land-grant schools in the second tier have made it into the inner circle of the research university, as signaled by membership in the American Association of Universities, and others are trying. Regional state universities in the third tier run into structural problems: for example, the reluctance by state educational leaders to allow California State University (CSU) campuses to offer doctoral degrees, which are generally reserved for the research universities in the University of California (UC) system. But this doesn't keep students at San José State from demanding an education that is as much like Berkeley as they can get. Given the vulnerability of universities to consumer pressure and the ingenuity of university presidents in pursuing institutional mobility, it would be risky to bet that these institutions will not continue to evolve toward the research university model.

Faculty members are another important factor pushing hard in this direction. A hefty proportion of the faculty in third-tier universities are graduates of doctoral programs from first-tier universities. This is a simple consequence of the status order of higher education, where advanced graduate education is concentrated at the top while undergraduate education is concentrated at the bottom. Thus most professors experience severe downward mobility when they graduate and take their first academic positions. Their preference in resolving this status loss is generally to move up the ladder and return to a position at a research university, but since the math clearly shows that this is unlikely, a second-best option is to increase the liberal content and graduate orientation of the institution they are in. (We'll explore this phenomenon in more depth in chapter 8.) Thus the ambitions of students, faculty, and administrators in third-tier institutions all converge in a conspiracy to drive these universities to pursue the brass ring.

TRIUMPH OF FORMALISM: VOCATIONAL PURPOSE, LIBERAL CONTENT

One conclusion we can draw from the story I'm telling in this chapter is this: professional education may be the biggest recurring loser in the history of American higher education. Responding to the rhythms of the educational status order, the professional keeps surging forward as the central thrust of new colleges and then retreating, as new institutions revert to the liberal norm.[32] Another way of putting this is that consumers got their way, time and time again. Social mobility continually trumped social efficiency. Lawmakers kept trying to push students into vocational colleges and students kept demanding and getting access to the liberal education and university structure they wanted, since these offered them the widest array of social opportunities.

Yet there is one way in which vocationalism has emerged as an increasingly dominant factor in American education at all levels: in shaping the system's purpose. In elementary, secondary, and higher education in the United States, practical education has indeed come to be dominant, but primarily in the broad realm of purpose rather than the contained realm of curriculum. The process of shifting educational purposes toward the practical has been going on in American education at all levels over the last 150 years. If you examine closely the sources I cited earlier in support of the proposition that higher education has become more professional, they are actually making a case for the dominance of professional purpose more than professional practice.[33]

The students who pursue higher education and the lawmakers who subsidize higher education disagree about the social function of this institution. Students see it as a private good, which helps them achieve social mobility, and the lawmakers see it as a public good, which promotes social efficiency. But they are in perfect agreement on one key point: they both value it primarily for its practical economic benefits. One focuses on individual outcomes and the other on collective outcomes, but for both parties, higher ed is all about preparing people for work. Its purpose, they agree, is vocational. The difference is that students see a liberal program of studies rather than a vocational program of studies as the most effective way to achieve this vocational goal.

Just because practical purposes have come to infuse American education at all levels does not mean that the content of higher education is also becoming more practical. On the contrary, as I have shown, higher education is liberalizing professional schools and staffing them with disciplinary theorists. At the same time that the purpose of education is becoming more practical, the content of education is becoming more liberal. This pattern is not as contradictory as it seems. As Turner points out, the same consumer pressure that promotes credential accumulation over learning also promotes general over specialized education, since general education is what opens up the most possibilities and defers the longest the need to put all your eggs in one vocational basket. Vocational education has always carried with it a degree of specialization that can easily turn into a dead end, as we have seen with high school vocational education programs, which too often have prepared people for jobs that no longer exist. The liberalization of professional education is in part driven by the contest mobility system of keeping your options open. But in part it's also driven by the realization that too much specialization is dangerous, that the best preparation for work may be a liberal education, and that specialized training is more efficiently provided on the job than in the university.

Suffice it to say that the growing power of the economistic vision of higher education has dramatically distorted the teaching and learning process, by focusing students' attention on the extrinsic rewards that come from acquiring an academic credential and thus undermining the incentive to learn. The result is a rising culture of credentialism and consumerism in both lower and higher education in the United States, where the emphasis is on the exchange value of education rather than its use value. Credentialism manages to empty the quest for liberal learning of much of its learning. What we end up with, then, is an increasingly liberal *form* of education even in professional schools and doctoral programs—the opposite of what much of the literature has been telling us. But this expanded sphere of liberal education has been drained of liberal *content* by the same vocational purposes that brought about this expansion in the first place.

Therefore, maybe what we have is a case of formalism playing itself out at two levels in higher education. At one level, we have liberal content masquerading as professional education, where the practicality of the education rides on its ability to land you a job rather than to teach you vocational skills. But at another level, we have a system that offers students little inducement to learn this liberal content, because their attention is focused on what they can buy with their educational credentials rather than how they can apply their knowledge. So liberal education has succeeded in colonizing professional education, but credentialism has turned this liberal education back toward vocational goals. The content is liberal, but credentialism means that the content doesn't really matter. The results for higher education can be rather depressing. Historian Laurence Veysey depicts it impact on the early twentieth-century university this way: "It would only slightly caricature the situation to conclude that the most important function of the American professor lay in posing requirements sufficiently difficult to give college graduates a sense of pride, yet not so demanding as to deny the degree to anyone who pledged four years of his parents' resources and his own time in residence at an academic institution."[34]

5

BALANCING ACCESS AND ADVANTAGE

In the previous chapter, we looked at one important tension in the American system of higher education, between professional education and liberal education. In the process, we saw that the driving force behind this tension was a more fundamental tension between education as a public good and education as a private good. Whereas government policy makers were seeking to frame college as a public good, to provide economically productive knowledge and skill that promotes the general welfare of society, student consumers were pursuing college enrollment as a private good, to give them credentials that advance their individual chances for social mobility. And in this contest for the soul of the system, consumers won. For them, liberal education at a full-service university provided the broadest array of opportunities for vocational success

In this chapter, we look more closely at the nature of this group of educational consumers I have been talking about. In particular, we examine the core tension within this group. They all want the higher education system to provide them with invidious distinctions that will mark them off from the pack and enhance their ability to compete for social position. But since they start from different inherited social positions, they are seeking from college fundamentally different social outcomes—either to gain social access or to preserve social advantage.

In a political democracy, people demand access to social opportunity. And, since schooling has come to be the primary way we decide who gets which job, this means gaining greater access to schooling at ever higher levels of the educational system. At the same time, however, in a liberal economy, where a high degree of social inequality is the norm, people who enjoy social advantages are eager to preserve these advantages and pass them on to their children. And, since we tend to award the best jobs to those with the best education, this means providing these children with privileged access to the most rewarding levels of schooling.

What happens if you put the two elements together? You find that, when access to schooling increases, so does the stratification of schooling. More students come in at the bottom of the system in order to gain social access, and the system keeps expanding upward in order to preserve social advantage. Levels of education rise but social differences remain the same. We want a society that allows us to have things both ways—equality and inequality, access and advantage—and our educational system is what makes this possible.

In this chapter, I explore how we can understand American higher education as the crowning achievement of a dynamic that has run through the historical expansion of American schooling over the last 200 years. The basic pattern has been this. At the starting point, one group has access to a level of education that is largely denied to another group. The outsiders exert pressure to gain greater access to this level, which democratically elected leaders eventually feel compelled to grant. But the insiders feel threatened by the loss of social advantage that greater access would bring, so they press to preserve that advantage. How does the system accomplish this? Through two simple mechanisms. First, at the level where access is expanding, it stratifies schooling into curricular tracks. This means that the newcomers fill the lower tracks while the old-timers occupy the upper tracks. Second, for the previously advantaged group it expands access to schooling at the next higher level. So the system expands access to one level of schooling while simultaneously stratifying that level and opening up the next level.

This process has gone through three cycles in the history of U.S.

education. When the common school movement created a system of universal elementary schooling in the second quarter of the nineteenth century, it also created a selective public high school at the top of the system. Then, when elementary grades filled up near the end of the century and demand increased for wider access to high school, the system opened the doors to this institution. But at the same it introduced curriculum tracks and set off a surge of college enrollments. And when high schools filled by the middle of the twentieth century, the system opened access to higher education by creating a range of new nonselective colleges and universities to absorb the influx. This preserved the exclusivity of the older institutions, whose graduates then started pursuing postgraduate degrees in large numbers.

When you think about it, this is an example of the brilliant way in which liberal democracies manage to satisfy conflicting demands from competing constituencies. Schools allow both rising access and continuing advantage. They allow outsiders into the zone of educational advantage. And at the same time they allow insiders to barricade themselves in the upper tracks of this zone, while simultaneously allowing them to pour into the new zone of educational advantage at the next higher level of the system. Educational access steadily grows, average levels of schooling keep rising, and the relative advantage among social groups remains the same. The system of schooling thus provides something for everyone. Some people can pursue the chance to get ahead and others the chance to stay ahead. Every time you raise the floor, you also raise the ceiling. The German sociologist Ulrich Bech calls this process the "elevator effect."[1] The American musician Paul Simon depicts it this way:

> It's apartment house sense
> It's like apartment house rents
> Remember: One man's ceiling
> Is another man's floor.[2]

In what follows, I first explore how the role of the consumer is in competition with the policy maker in American education. Then I explore how this access-advantage dynamic played out in the history of American schooling across three stages of expanding enrollment and increasing stratification: the explosion in enrollments in elementary, then secondary, then higher education in the last two centuries. Finally, I examine how the interaction between public and private colleges in the United States has helped reinforce the extreme stratification of the higher education system.

The Background: How Consumers Came to Trump Policy Makers

Educational consumers are a different breed from educational policy makers. For one thing, as we saw in the last chapter, policy makers see education as a public good, whose benefits are shared by all. Consumers see it as a private good, a way for individuals and families to get ahead or stay ahead in the social hierarchy. For another, policy makers are deliberately trying to change education in order to make it effective at solving urgent social problems. Consumers are only trying to use education to serve their own personal needs. They're not trying to institute change in the system, but the accumulation of their individual actions nonetheless has an enormous impact on the system's form and function. This impact is no less significant because it is unintended.

A third difference is that policy makers focus their attention on promoting learning whereas consumers don't. Policy makers see education as a mechanism for socialization, in which students learn the skills, knowledge, and attitudes that are required to address major social issues, such as by constructing capable citizens or training productive workers. In contrast, educational consumers approach schooling as a mechanism that allocates people to social positions. For them, its primary function is not learning but credentialing. By accumulating the tokens of education—grades, credits, and degrees—consumers can gain access to social opportunity and can preserve social advantage.

How do consumers shape education? Through two primary mechanisms: consumer actions and political pressure. By consumer actions I mean the choices that individuals and their families take in pursuing their positional interests though education. This includes whether to pursue school at all and at what level; which kind of school to attend; what program or curriculum stream to pursue within a school; whether to terminate or continue schooling at a particular stage; and how much time, effort, money, and forgone income to invest in schooling at one stage or another. Education forces consumers to make choices, and in aggregate these choices can exert a powerful impact on which programs and tracks and schools are going to expand or contract at a given time. This impact is particularly evident in higher education, where enrollment is voluntary and the range of choices is greater. As these choices pile up, the shape of the system changes accordingly.

The other mechanism by which consumers shape education is political pressure. By this I mean that educational consumers are also citizens, who can exert influence through sheer force of numbers in the political arena. It is in the nature of societies in general and liberal democracies in particular that the less advantaged tend to outnumber the more advantaged. The people who are enjoying the benefits of higher levels of education are fewer than the people who have lower levels of education. The mathematics of democratic politics means that when large numbers of outsiders seek greater access to the educational levels dominated by smaller numbers of insiders, they can eventually accumulate enough votes to support their demand. But at the same time, the insiders are in a good position to defend their privileges. They may not be able to head off forever the demand by others for greater access, but their positions of power—as owners, professionals, managers, and political leaders—mean that they are able to structure the new, more accessible educational system in a way that favors them. So they stratify the new zone of educational access such that outsiders enroll in the lower tracks, preserving the upper tracks for their own children, and they also send their children in greater numbers to schooling at the next higher level of the system. Each group uses its political clout to gain something from the process, and the net result is the aforementioned elevator effect, an increase in schooling without a change in the relative social position of the two groups.

This is an argument based on a vision of schooling as a private good rather than a public good, as a medium of selection rather than a medium of socialization. My focus in this book is on schooling rather than education. I'm not arguing that learning doesn't matter or that education doesn't take place in schools. I'm only arguing that you can understand the development of school systems in liberal democracies without recourse to ideas such as education or learning. These things may be happening in schools, but they are not necessary for understanding how the system of schooling has come to take the form that it has. My point is that consumers of schooling have been less interested in learning than in gaining or holding social position. And in the history of schooling in the United States, the consumer has been king.

In order to illustrate this point, we now turn to the history of American schooling. In doing so, I look at three periods of educational expansion in the United States: the emergence of universal primary schooling in the early nineteenth century, the sudden explosion of high school enrollments at the turn of the twentieth century, and the surge in higher education after the Second World War.

The Emergence of Universal Primary Schooling in the United States

The creation of universal schooling in the United States is the exception that proves the rule. It is the one major educational policy effort in American history that succeeded in meeting its goals, and the consumer did not play a significant role in the process. Once set in motion, however, the American educational system took on a life of its own, and the role of the consumer emerged quickly as a major and eventually dominant factor.

As in most other countries, the United States established a system of universal schooling for the purpose of building a nation.[3] In the early nineteenth century, the country was in crisis. It was a new republic in a world where republics had a history of not lasting very long.

From ancient Rome to Renaissance Florence, republics over time had tended to veer toward tyranny. Civic virtue gives way to individual self-interest, and those with the most power and money take charge of political life. The founders of the American republic were acutely aware of this history and tried to build into the U.S. Constitution safeguards that would ward off such tendencies. But they understood that—without a citizenry that was imbued with dedication to preserving republican community and a willingness to put aside personal gain—the republic was in danger. So from the very beginning, the founders talked about public education as the central mechanism for producing citizens with these necessary dispositions. But the form that education took in the first three decades of the nineteenth century fell short of the ideal. In American cities, there was a move to create free publicly operated schools for those who were too poor to provide for their children's education. But this only exacerbated social differences, leading to a public system for paupers and a private system for the privileged.

In the 1820s, this problem came to a head because of the sudden surge of the free-market economy in the United States. This was the time when investments by states and by the federal government in canals and turnpikes spurred a dramatic growth in commerce and the emergence of rapidly expanding regional and national markets for crops and manufactures. This growth in markets offered great opportunities for producers to get rich selling to distant buyers and for workers to gain freedom from patriarchal authority. But it also posed great risks for producers to be put out of business by distant competitors and for workers to lose social and economic security. And all of this presented a serious danger for the republic. The surging market economy promoted self-interest over community interest and led to sharp increases in differences between the rich and the poor.

Out of this social, economic, and political crisis came the common school movement, which sought to produce a system of public schools that would be free and universal. The idea was not just to provide schooling for everyone but also to create a system where that schooling would take place in a way that everyone in a community would attend the same school. These schools were supposed to solve the crisis of the early republic by reconciling the new polity with the market economy. To succeed, this system was supposed to bring together all the young people of the community, give them a common educational experience, and instill in them a sense of civic virtue so they would be able to function as self-interested actors in the market while still remaining community-minded citizens of the republic.

This model would only work, however, if the reformers were able to induce middle- and upper-class families to enroll their children in the new schools. In short, they had to overcome the stigma of pauperism that marked public education. They had to make the common schools truly common. And to do this, they deployed a very effective form of inducement. At the same time that the reformers created the common school, to provide elementary education for the many, they also created the public high school, which was to provide secondary education for the few. For example, when policy makers in Philadelphia created Central High School as part of the city's new common school system, they made it an extraordinarily uncommon institution. It was located in the best part of town, with a marble facade, teachers called professors, and a curriculum that was better than most private academies and the equal of many colleges. To enroll there, students needed to pass an entrance exam. They also needed to be enrolled in the common grammar schools. Private school students were not welcome. This kind of selective inducement proved effective in luring middle-class families to start sending their children to the new public schools.[4]

The common school movement was remarkably successful. Not only did it create a system of universal schooling at the elementary level but it also managed to blunt the social divisions and self-interested behaviors of the surging market economy. It drew everyone into the community school and there imbued them with the spirit of republican citizenship. And key to its success was the high school. This is the institution that helped make the common school common, but it's also the institution where enrollment was thoroughly uncommon.

So the kind of tension I am talking about—between access and advantage—was there at the very beginning of the American public school system. The only way the system could be broadly inclusive at one level was for it to be narrowly exclusive at the next higher level. The two elements were inseparable from the start.

The Expansion of High School Enrollment

Once launched in the early nineteenth century, the high school attracted the attention of families who were thinking of it less as publicly minded citizens than as self-interested consumers. With everyone now having access to elementary schooling, the high school was the central zone of educational distinction. People who went there were special, though Philadelphia was an extreme case; for example, as late as 1880 only 1 percent of the students attending the city's public schools were enrolled in high school. High school enrollment was more common in smaller cities and towns, but nonetheless gaining admission to this institution was a remarkable achievement; graduating put you in the educational elite. As a result, high school emerged as an attractive cultural commodity, a way to mark your children off from the pack. And enrollments in high school came overwhelmingly from the middle and upper-middle classes. They were more likely to have the cultural capital needed to pass the entrance exam, and they were best able to afford the opportunity cost of sending a teenager to school instead of to work.

So what happened next? In retrospect it seems obvious: other families started to demand access to the high school. After all, it was a public institution supported with public funds, and to deny access to qualified students was simply undemocratic. This spurred commentary in the press about the high school as an aristocratic institution unsuited to a republic. In a famous case in 1859, the citizens of Beverly, Massachusetts, voted on these grounds to disband their local high school.[5] The more common response, however, was to spur demand for greater access, which got gradually stronger as the number of students in the primary grades grew and expanded into grammar school.

Toward the end of the century, completion of grammar school—the first eight grades of the school system—was becoming the norm. By 1900, the average American twenty-year-old had eight years of schooling.[6] For these students, the next step in the educational ladder was high school. To deny them access would be to cut them off from the American Dream.

With the pressure building in the last part of the nineteenth century, the politics of secondary education became a zone of conflict. Cities tried imposing quotas to allow students from all geographical areas access to high school, but this change in regional allocation did nothing to increase supply. Finally, in the 1880s city leaders began to give in to the pressure and started opening new secondary schools. Initially, they were often set up as manual training schools, which left the original high schools with a monopoly on academic secondary education. But by the first decade of the twentieth century, these new institutions had quickly evolved under political pressure into comprehensive high schools, each serving its own geographical area.

Before this expansion, the city high school was an extraordinarily selective and elevated institution. For example, with a population of 850,000, Philadelphia in 1880 had only one high school for all the boys in the city and another for the girls. But the huge surge of growth at the turn of the century made the uncommon high school increasingly common. Nationally, the number of high schools rose from 2,500 in 1890 to more than 14,000 in 1920, and enrollments grew from 200,000 to two million.[7]

In the face of this flood of new high school students, what could the old high school's traditional beneficiaries, middle-class families, do in order to preserve educational advantage for their children? There were initial efforts to keep the newcomers in special schools, like manual training schools or schools focused on preparing students for industrial and clerical work. But by the First World War, these efforts at containment had failed in the face of huge pressure from former outsiders (reinforced by labor unions and political progressives), who demanded access not to a segregated vocational school but to a real full-service public high school.

The result of these contradictory pressures was a new form of school that came to be the model for how the system could combine the urges for access and advantage in a single institution: the tracked comprehensive high school. This school drew an increasingly broad socioeconomic array of students from a single region of a city and educated them within the walls of the same educational organization. But once there, the school sorted these students into a series of distinct academic programs that were organized into a clear hierarchy. This was in striking contrast with the nineteenth-century high school, where all students tended to take the same curriculum. Now there was the industrial program, which prepared students for work in factories; the mechanical program, which prepared them for engineering and skilled trades; the commercial program, which prepared them for clerical roles in business; and the academic program, which provided a liberal education that prepared them for college and future roles in management and the professions. As a result, working-class families gained access to the once elite realm of high school education, but found themselves largely relegated to the lower tracks of this institution. At the same time, middle-class families preserved the elite academic niche within the high school for themselves, and they also started sending their children in large numbers to college.

The Expansion of College Enrollment

With these new institutional arrangements in place, high school attendance went through an astonishingly rapid period of growth. Enrollments doubled every decade from 1890 to 1940, increasing from 200,000 to 6.6 million.[8] Between 1900 and 1940, the proportion of fourteen- to seventeen-year-olds attending high school rose from 11 percent to 71 percent.[9] During the same period, college enrollments also grew rapidly, rising from a quarter million to 1.5 million, and the proportion of the college-age population attending college rose from 2 percent to 9 percent.[10]

So in the early twentieth century, high school attendance became the norm for working-class and middle-class families, and college attendance became the norm for upper-middle-class families.[11] For each group, this level of education emerged as what these families needed if their children were going to have a good chance to get ahead or stay ahead. And by the U.S. entry into the Second World War, high schools were filling up. The large majority of eligible students were already enrolled, so working-class consumers increasingly turned their attention toward college as the new zone of educational advantage. Attending high school could keep your children from falling beyond in the competition for social position, but at this stage only college could help them get ahead.

As a result, the demand for access to the elite realm of higher education grew strong. Especially in the wake of the war, when so many soldiers had sacrificed so much, to deny such access was politically impossible. The GI Bill provided funds for veterans to attend college, which gave a big incentive for colleges to expand to meet the new demand. Enrollments shot up from 1.5 million in 1940 to 2.4 million in 1950. But long after the veterans had moved on, the rate of enrollment increase kept accelerating, with the biggest surge occurring in the 1960s. College enrollments reached 3.6 million in 1960, 8 million in 1970, and 11.6 million in 1980.[12] At the end of this forty-year period, the number of students attending college was eight times higher than it had been at the start of the war.

This was an extraordinary expansion of educational opportunity in a very short time. But the pattern established during the expansion of the high school repeated itself with the expansion of the college. The newcomers did not flood into the same institutions that had become the home of middle-class students in the years between the wars. Instead, the higher education system created a series of new lower-level institutions to make room for the influx, leaving the college's core middle-class constituency safely protected in institutions that, instead of becoming more accessible in the face of greater demand, chose to became more exclusive.

Until the 1940s, American colleges had admitted students with little concern for academic merit or selectivity, and this was true not only for state universities but also for the private universities now considered as the pinnacle of the system. If you met certain minimal academic requirements and could pay the tuition, you were admitted. But in the postwar years, a sharp divide emerged in the system between the established colleges and universities, which dragged their feet about expanding enrollments and instead became increasingly selective, and the new institutions, which expanded rapidly by admitting nearly everyone who applied.

What were these new institutions that welcomed the newcomers? Often, existing public universities would set up branch campuses in other regions of the state, which eventually became independent institutions. Former normal schools, set up in the nineteenth century as high school–level institutions for preparing teachers, had evolved into teachers colleges in the early twentieth century, and by the middle of the century they had evolved into full-service state colleges and universities serving regional populations. A number of new urban college campuses also emerged during this period, aimed at students who would commute from home to pursue programs that would prepare them for midlevel white-collar jobs. And the biggest players in the new lower tier of American higher education were community colleges, which provided two-year programs that allowed students to enter low-level white-collar jobs or transfer to the university. Community colleges quickly became the largest provider of college instruction in the country. By 1980, they accounted for about 40 percent of all college enrollments in the United States.[13]

These new colleges and universities had several characteristics in common. Compared to their predecessors, they focused on undergraduate education, prepared students for immediate entry into the workforce, drew students from nearby, cost little, and admitted almost anyone. For all these reasons, especially the last, they also occupied a position in the college hierarchy that was markedly lower. Just as secondary education expanded by only allowing the newcomers access to the lower tiers of the new comprehensive high school, so higher education expanded by only allowing newcomers access to the lower tiers of the newly stratified structure of the tertiary system.

As a result, the newly expanded and stratified system of higher education protected upper-middle-class students attending the older selective institutions from the lower-middle-class students attending regional and urban universities and from the working-class students attending community colleges. At the same time, these upper-middle-class students started pouring into graduate programs in law, medicine, business, and engineering, which quickly became the new zone of educational advantage.

Data on attainment of BA degrees by family income show that the huge expansion of access to higher education also expanded educational advantage. Between 1965 and 2013, the proportion of twenty-four-year-olds who gained a BA rose from 6 percent to 9 percent for families in the bottom quartile by income, but the proportion rose from 40 percent to 77 percent for families in the top quartile. This means that the top group was about seven times as likely to gain a degree at the start of this period, but the edge grew to about nine times as likely by the end.[14] We see the same pattern if we look at degree attainment for students who entered college. Between 1970 and 2013, the proportion of students from the bottom quartile who completed a BA stayed about the same, going from 22 percent to 21 percent, while those from the top quartile nearly doubled, rising from 55 percent to 99 percent. This means that the degree completion advantage for the top group grew from 33 percentage points to 78 percentage points.[15]

As you can see, pressures for access and pressures for advantage have radically shaped the evolution of the American system of education. It's a case of how educational systems in liberal democracies perform a kind of magic trick. They can continually expand educational opportunity without reducing social inequality. They can increase educational access while still preserving educational advantage. Every time they raise the floor, they also raise the ceiling. In this sense, these educational systems are amazingly effective. They give something to everyone without the need to make fundamental changes in the allocation of social power and privilege. The social structure remains the same, and its legitimacy floats high and dry on a rising tide of schooling.

6

PRIVATE ADVANTAGE,
PUBLIC IMPACT

One of the peculiar aspects of the history of American higher education is that private colleges preceded public. Another, which in part follows from the first, is that private colleges are also more prestigious. Nearly everywhere else in the world, state-supported and -governed universities occupy the pinnacle of the national system, while private institutions play a small and subordinate role, supplying degrees of less distinction and serving students of less ability. But in the United States, the top private universities produce more research, gain more academic citations, attract better faculty and students, and graduate more leaders of industry, government, and the professions. According to the 2014 Shanghai rankings, sixteen of the top twenty-five universities in the United States are private, and the concentration is even higher at the top of this list, where private institutions make up eight of the top ten.[1]

In this chapter, I explore the peculiar role that private institutions have played in shaping the American system of higher education, the nature of the advantages enjoyed by these institutions, and the quality of their impact on the public colleges and universities that enroll the large majority of students.

Discerning the Difference

The term "private university" has a distinctive meaning in the United States. For much of the developing world today, in places such as India and Brazil, private universities are for-profit institutions that have emerged recently in response to the demand for higher education that was not being met by the older and more prestigious public sector. The United States has a for-profit sector as well, which has been rapidly growing since 2000, but it is still a rather small part of the whole, accounting for less than 10 percent of enrollments.[2] In Europe, private universities have existed for years, largely under religious auspices, but they receive state funding and submit to state regulation in much the same way as public universities. In the United States, a private university is a not-for-profit institution, which has a corporate charter from the state but which does not receive state appropriations for its core functions and does not submit to state governance. Private universities do benefit from government funding in important ways, through research grants, student loans and scholarships, and the tax subsidy for private donations. But such funding does not pay for faculty salaries, buildings, and other central costs of running the institution.

For most of the history of American higher education, however, the distinction between public and private institutions was anything but clear. Until the Dartmouth College decision, it was reasonable to assume that the grant of a state corporate charter for any institution, whether a college or a for-profit company, made it more or less public. Only when the Supreme Court in 1819 ruled that states had no right to intrude on the autonomy of any chartered corporation did state governments start establishing colleges and universities that were clearly subject to state control.

But the differences between public and private remained murky until the twentieth century. This was particularly the case with respect to funding. Until about 1910, state funding for public colleges and universities was neither regular nor reliable, based as it was on specific appropriations and tied to particular sources of funds (such as lotteries or public lands). Only at this point, as the system was institutionalizing around the university model, did states start providing regular annual appropriations to give basic support for public institutions.[3] Before then, being public did not guarantee state funding and being private did not bar such funding.

Private colleges did not start calling themselves private until rather late in the game, typically after they had already failed to get the state funds they were seeking. Only at this stage did they start bragging about their independent status, in the hope that this would be a lure for donors.[4] In the eighteenth and nineteenth centuries, private colleges frequently received government funds. Their much-vaunted independence was a late invention, which leaders then retroactively ascribed to a past when their institutions actually had neither sought nor attained this condition. For example, in an 1873 speech opposing establishment of a proposed federally funded national university, Harvard's president Charles W. Eliot grandly asserted the value of his college's stalwart autonomy: "Our ancestors well understood the principle that to make a people free and self-reliant, it is necessary to let them take care of themselves."[5] What he failed to mention is that, during its first 150 years, Harvard (which was founded in 1636) accepted more than 100 appropriations from the colonial government of Massachusetts, thus demonstrating that it was anything but self-sufficient. And this kind of public subsidy continued in the nineteenth century. Between 1814 and 1823, Harvard received $100,000 from the commonwealth—$1.7 million in current dollars. And it was not alone. Lots of colleges were eager to be on the public dole. Bowdoin and Williams each received $30,000 ($500,000 in current dollars) from the same state appropriation. This pattern continued to the end of the century, when, for example, Columbia received $140,000 and University of Pennsylvania received $287,000 from their state governments ($3.6 million and $7.4 million, respectively, in current dollars).[6]

Fortunately for the private colleges, just when states were beginning to bar the door to public subsidies, their private fund-raising capabilities were expanding. In part this was the result of the booming economy after the Civil War, which increased the wealth and generosity of alumni. This was particularly important as a way to replace support from religious denominations, which was declining substantially in the latter part of the century.[7] In part it emerged from the rise of super-rich philanthropists in the Gilded Age, when people like Ezra Cornell, Johns Hopkins, John D. Rockefeller, Cornelius Vanderbilt, and Leland Stanford were able to provide huge endowments for new universities and buy naming rights for older colleges.[8] And in part it came from the growing sophistication of institutional fund-raising efforts by college presidents.

As he was in so many other areas, Harvard's Eliot was in the vanguard of institutional fund-raisers. During his forty years as president, which ended in 1909, he developed a financial system of institutional advancement, which he summarized this way: "In the competition between American universities, and between American and foreign universities, those universities will inevitably win which have the largest amounts of free money."[9] By "free money" he meant endowed funds that were unrestricted by the donor, that left the university free to spend the earnings as it wished, and that also freed it from primary reliance of student tuition. To reassure donors, the university must manage its operations like a prudent business. But quite unlike a business—and this was central to his strategy—the university should always run a deficit in order to maintain a perpetual need for more donations.[10]

In the twentieth century, this vision of the central role of endowments in enhancing the competitive standing of universities became the credo of ambitious university presidents across the country, especially those in the private sector. And as the wealthiest of the bunch, Harvard kept faith with the Eliot's principles. When I was applying for admission to Harvard in 1965, I encountered a line from its marketing brochure that has stuck in my mind ever since and that neatly captures Eliot's vision: "Wealth, like age, does not make a university great. But it helps."[11]

Considering the Relative Scale

So in the history of American higher education, private colleges came first, but since the Civil War, the greatest growth was in the public sector. States were creating their own universities, land-grant colleges, and normal schools, and at the same time they were growing increasingly reluctant to provide public funds for private institutions. However, in spite of this pattern of public-sector growth, the role of the private sector in the United States has remained very large. In 1921 (the first year for which there are reliable statistics about colleges by type of control), 644 of the 1,162 institutions of higher education in the United States were private, 55 percent of the total.[12] Since then the number of institutions in both sectors has gradually risen, but until midcentury the rate of growth in the private sector was consistently higher. By 1950, the private proportion had risen to 65 percent (1,210 out of 1,851). And this proportion remained the same over the next sixty years, during which the number of institutions continued to grow. In 2013, 3,103 out of 4,726 institutions were private, or 66 percent.[13]

Although the private sector has remained dominant in number of institutions, it has lost out over time in the proportion of total student enrollments. But this shift took a remarkably long time to develop. One reason is that, although private colleges in the nineteenth century were usually very small, the colleges with the largest enrollments were in fact private. In 1880, two-thirds of the largest universities in the United States were under private control. Amherst College was as big as the University of Wisconsin, and Yale was bigger than the University of Michigan.[14] Getting established first gave them a big advantage in drawing power, especially in a century when the funding for public institutions was far from secure. This changed in the early twentieth century, giving public enrollments a boost. But still it was not until 1931 that total public enrollments first inched past the private sector, and the lead kept changing hands until 1952, after which the public sector solidified its dominant position.[15] Then the Cold War surge in public funding for higher education took charge, accelerating the expansion of public enrollments. In 1961, 62 percent of 4.1 million college students were in public institutions. In 1971, it was 76 percent of 8.9 million. For the next three decades, the proportion stayed around 78 percent as enrollments grew to 15.9 million. Then in 2011, largely because of a surge of enrollments in the newly expanding for-profit colleges, the public proportion dropped to 72 percent of 21 million students.[16]

The Private Advantage

In the highly stratified market-based system of higher education in the United States, expanding enrollment for a public university is a mixed blessing. During the Cold War period of greatest public growth, when state appropriations tended to rise with enrollments, admitting more students allowed public universities to sharply increase faculty hiring, building construction, and investment in research facilities. But at the same time, it made them less exclusive. Recall that the system awards the highest standing to the institutions with the most restrictive admissions, those in the top two tiers: elite research universities and land-grant research universities.[17] The highest-ranked public universities, such as Berkeley and Michigan, are considerably more selective in admissions than the land-grant or regional public universities, but it is politically impossible for them to be as selective as the privates. And this is particularly true for undergraduate admissions.

Picture how difficult it is for a flagship state university to deny the applications of large numbers of state residents. Yes, there are public alternatives that are more accessible, such as community colleges and regional universities, but consumers know that research institutions offer the best social opportunities, so they apply for admission there in greater numbers and face increasing rates of rejection. For example, between the mid-1990s and 2014, the rate of undergraduate admissions at the top four campuses of the University of California dropped by more than half, with the University of California, Los Angeles (UCLA), most recently admitting only 16 percent of California residents who applied.[18] This decline caused major political problems for top campuses, even though the rate of in-state admissions across all nine UC campuses was a quite accessible 61 percent. By and large, students could get into one of the campuses, even if it was not the one they wanted. By contrast, Stanford in 2014 admitted 5 percent of those who applied. Of the 100 American universities with the lowest undergraduate acceptance rates in 2013, eighty were private institutions. The only public institutions in the top fifty were the federal military academies, Berkeley, and UCLA.[19]

In the balancing act between populism and elitism that charac-
terizes the American system of higher education, public research
universities need to shore up their populist credentials by remaining
more accessible than private universities. The latter, buffered from
political pressure for greater access, can afford to adopt a more elitist
stance. And this stance in turn gives them a boost in university rank.
Why? Because selectivity is a factor in most of the measures used by
various ranking systems. That is particularly true for the criteria used
by *U.S. News and World Report* in establishing its influential rankings
of American colleges. Selectivity influences criteria such as academic
reputation, acceptance rate, class rank, average SAT/ACT scores, student retention, student-faculty ratio, and graduation rate.[20] Paralleling
the numbers I gave earlier from the Shanghai rankings but in more
dramatic form, *U.S. News and World Report* in 2015 showed American
private universities with a huge advantage over their public counterparts. In the category of national universities, privates accounted for
all of the top ten, nineteen of the top twenty (Berkeley squeaked in
at the twentieth slot), twenty-five of the top thirty, and thirty-four of
the top fifty.[21]

Another way to think about selectivity is to reverse the direction.
Instead of examining how choosy colleges are in admitting students,
we can look at how choosy students are in accepting college offers
of admission. Consumer preference is particularly important to consider in a market-based system such as American higher education,
where the consumer is so powerful. A study by Caroline Hoxby and
colleagues sought to measure the revealed preference of student consumers in an ingenious manner, by examining what action they took
when admitted to more than one college. From the choices made by
the 3,200 students in the sample (who came from forty-three states),
the researchers constructed a rank ordering of American institutions
of higher education according to consumer preference. This ranking
is even more extremely skewed toward private universities. Of the top
100 institutions in the list, eighty were private. At the high end of the
market, American consumers just love the private sector.[22]

Private universities not only gain advantage from their elitist admissions policy, but they also use this to shift the weight of their institutional efforts away from undergraduate teaching and toward graduate education and research. For example, compare the two primary competitors in the San Francisco Bay area. In the 2014–15 academic year, Stanford had 3,700 undergraduate students and 5,400 graduate students.[23] Berkeley had 27,100 undergraduates and 10,500 graduates.[24] So Berkeley is four times as large as Stanford, and 71 percent of its students are undergraduates, compared to 41 percent for Stanford. This means that Berkeley professors spend a lot more time teaching large, lower-level courses and less time working with graduate students and doing research. In turn this means that the private school will have an edge in other measures of institutional quality in the research-university horse race, such as the number of PhD students per professor and average research funding per professor.

Because private research universities are more focused on graduate education and research, they tend to dominate the rankings of graduate programs across a wide array of domains. For example, according to *U.S. News and World Report*, in economics, physics, business, and law, all of the top five graduate programs are at private universities. The privates also account for four of the top five programs in history, English, math, medicine, biology, chemistry, and engineering; three of the top five in computer science; and two of the top five in psychology and sociology.[25] This kind of private dominance in a wide range of graduate programs tends to be self-perpetuating, because the top departments tend to hire faculty who are graduates of other top departments.

Val Burris did a study of hiring in all ninety-four programs in the United States that granted PhDs in sociology. He found that top-five departments hire 56 percent of their faculty from the pool of graduates from other top-five departments and only 9 percent from departments below the top twenty. Overall, the top five departments supplied one-third of the faculty for all ninety-four departments, and the top twenty supplied two-thirds. Because of the dominant position of the top departments in supplying faculty for the field, only 6 percent of faculty were upwardly mobile after graduation (i.e., were hired at a department that ranked higher than the one from which they graduated); 54 percent were downwardly mobile, and 40 percent stayed at the same level. As a result of this, departments at the top of the rankings tend to remain at the top over time, with minor fluctuations. In five different prestige rankings in sociology between 1957 and 1993, four departments (Chicago, Berkeley, Harvard, and Michigan) occupied a place in the top eight departments on every list and two others (Columbia and North Carolina) showed up on four out of five lists.[26] Sociology is unusual in that it's a field where public universities have managed to remain competitive at the highest level. But this study demonstrates that the best academic departments tend to maintain their position over time and that they produce a disproportionate number of faculty members for lower-ranking departments. As we have seen, in the large majority of fields across the full range of academic specialties, private universities dominate. The consequence is that private universities provide a disproportionate number of faculty for public institutions.

Roots of the Private Advantage

So what are the roots of the advantage that private universities enjoy in the American system of higher education? We have already explored one such advantage—that private institutions are able to make undergraduate programs smaller and more selective and thus focus more heavily on graduate instruction and research. In his classic analysis of the subject, "The American Private University," Edward Shils identifies three additional factors that give the edge to the private sector, which he calls sovereignty, affluence, and tradition. Let me say a little about each.

SOVEREIGNTY

Private universities have considerably more control over their fate than do their public counterparts. The president is accountable to a board of trustees, which owns the university, exercises fiduciary responsibility over it, and hires the president. This board, in turn, is made up of laypeople (usually not academics), who are typically alumni of the institution, ardent supporters, and, in more recent years, generous donors. As we saw in chapter 3, board membership shifted in the late nineteenth century away from clergy and toward people in business and the professions. Board members are either selected by the board itself or elected by alumni or some combination of the two.

The governance structure of public universities varies by state, but they are all subject to a board under the political authority of the state, either through a constitutional mandate or by statutory authority of the legislature. Board members may be appointed by the governor or other elected officials (subject to legislative approval or veto) or (rarely) elected by citizens. This board sets academic policy and establishes guidelines for fiscal management. Some state universities have their own boards, but it is more common that they are part of a state system of higher education whose board oversees all universities in the system. California, for example, has three systems—University of California (ten campuses), California State University (with twenty-three campuses), and the community college system (with 112 campuses). Each UC campus has its own chancellor, who is accountable to the president of the whole system, who in turn is accountable to the UC Board of Regents. California State University has a similar structure, but the system allows less autonomy for individual campuses.

Ask top administrators at private universities about autonomy, and they will complain about how much they are constrained by federal and state laws and regulations. But they will also exclaim about how much worse the situation is in the public sector. One source of trouble for the public university is the layers of authority and bureaucracy that you need to traverse in order get approval for decisions—from campus to system to board and to the governor and legislature. This does not make for an institution that is as fast on its feet as the private university, with its lean and local chain of command. Another source of trouble, of course, is politics. Any actions taken at the campus level—setting admission rates, tuition charges, program changes—have to take into account the broader implications of this action in the context of the political structure of the state and the climate of opinion among state lawmakers and voters. Private university leaders, in contrast, enjoy not only less bureaucracy but much less politics.

The final and perhaps most significant problem for academic leaders in the public sector is that (depending on the state) they are more or less heavily dependent on the governor and state legislature for the continuing funds required to run the university. As we will see in the following chapter, this funding can boom, as it briefly did during the Cold War, or go bust, as it did after 1989. But either way, it is a stream of money that you cannot depend on. In most states, higher education is the largest segment of the state's discretionary budget. While funding for elementary and secondary education is mandated by state constitutions, legislatures have leeway in determining how to fund higher education.[27] The result is huge variation in university funding between states and across time. From long experience with these fluctuating circumstances—and a 150-year history of public underfunding—public universities have developed strategies for gaining alternative sources of funding, primarily through tuition, donations, and research grants. But even here there are restrictions. Although the state is reluctant to fund public universities at the level they would like, it is also reluctant to authorize increases in tuition that will spur a public outcry. And there is also an unfortunate feedback effect: the more successful the public university is at raising alternative sources of support, the less the state feels compelled to provide public support.

So what are the benefits of the private university's greater autonomy? One benefit we have already seen, which is that, in the absence of state pressure to educate large numbers of undergraduates, it can get away with admitting only the strongest undergraduates applicants and concentrate efforts on graduate education and research. This in turn gives it a higher profile of academic excellence and research productivity and allows it to colonize public research universities with its own doctoral graduates.

Another benefit is that the private university can be much more nimble in pursuing new academic opportunities, developing new programs, and competing effectively in the evolving higher education market place. Not being compelled to work through many layers of bureaucracy or to please political masters, administrators and professors have more freedom to do what they want to advance both the interests of the institution and their own careers. The relative lack of red tape fosters a culture of entrepreneurship, which turns the university into a bubbling cauldron of self-directed activity driven by ambition. This is intensified because the private university is not able to rely on a steady stream of state funding but needs to generate its own support through the highly competitive pursuit of donors, grants, and tuition-paying students. A study of universities in Europe and the United States by Caroline Hoxby and associates shows that this mix of institutional autonomy and competition is strongly associated with higher rankings in the world ecology of higher education. They find that "each percentage of a university's budget that is from core government funds is associated with a decrease of 3.2 rank points in its Shanghai Index." Likewise, "Each percentage of a university's budget from competitive grants is associated with an increase of 6.5 rank points."[28] They also found that universities high in autonomy and competition also produced more research (as measured by number of patents).

AFFLUENCE

American private universities are much wealthier than their public-sector counterparts. And this wealth is itself concentrated in a few private universities at the top. Moody's rates the debt of more than 500 universities in the United States, which enroll about 80 percent of the four-year students in the country. In 2014, the ten universities with the most wealth (investments and cash) accounted for one-third of the wealth of the 500 institutions in the analysis. The top forty universities accounted for two-thirds of the total. And, of course, the schools at the top were mostly private.[29] If you look just at endowment, which is the more usual way to measure university wealth, these were the top ten universities for 2014:

Harvard	$35.9 billion
Yale	23.9
Stanford	21.4
Princeton	21.0
MIT	12.4
Northwestern	9.8
Michigan	9.7
Penn	9.6
Columbia	9.2
Notre Dame	8.0

Michigan was the only public university to make it into the top ten. Only thirteen public institutions made it into the top fifty. In addition there were three statewide public university systems in the top fifty, including University of Texas, Texas A&M, and University of California, each with multiple campuses.[30]

Those with the greatest wealth also tend to be those that raise the most money in a given year. In 2013, the top ten fund-raisers were all private universities, headed by Stanford at $931 million. In at number eleven was UCLA, with $420 million.[31] Donations to universities constitute a large share of total American philanthropy. One study showed that, "in 1994–95, the 400 largest charities alone raised $22.4 billion. . . . Of these 400 institutions, 151 were universities, raising almost $7 billion. This figure represents over half the total amount raised by higher education institutions ($12.4 billion)."[32]

Recall the bit of wisdom from the Harvard recruiting brochure: "Wealth, like age, does not make a university great. But it helps." It sure does. Let's count the ways. First, note that the wealthiest schools tend to top the rankings. Of the ten schools with the largest endowments (shown above), six are in the top ten American universities in the Shanghai rankings; all except Notre Dame are in the top twenty. Seven are among the top twenty universities in the world, and all seven of these are private institutions.[33]

Second, money can buy talent. University rankings depend heavily on the accomplishments of faculty, measured by such things as the dollar value of research grants they win, the number of scholarly citations gained by the research they publish, the awards they earn, the national boards they sit on, and the leadership positions they hold. And institutions that win high rankings this way can solidify their position by using this prestige to attract more top scholars. Institutional status is an important currency in the academic world. (At academic conferences, people look at the university affiliation shown on your name badge in order to see if you're someone who matters.) As a result, letterhead lust is rampant among academics seeking to enhance their careers. Name brands matter. (As an example: when I moved from Michigan State to Stanford a dozen years ago, I seemed to become a lot smarter overnight, as I started getting bombarded with invitations to join editorial boards, give speeches, write blurbs for books, and join projects. A pure letterhead effect.)

But rich schools not only offer prestige to attract faculty; they also offer higher salaries. On average, private colleges pay only a little more than public colleges, but that is because a large number of private liberal arts colleges are relatively poor. A more telling comparison is between salaries at the highest-paying institutions in the two sectors. In the 2013–14 academic year, average pay for full professors at the ten top-paying private universities ranged from $210,000 at Stanford to $186,000 at Princeton. The comparable range in the public sector was from $170,000 at UCLA to $145,000 at Virginia. On average across the top ten in each sector, professors at private universities were making $44,000 a year more, a private-sector advantage of 29 percent.[34] And this gap has been growing over time. One study shows that full professors at private research universities in 1980 had a pay advantage over their public counterparts of only 2 percent; but the gap grew to 20 percent in 1990 and to 29 percent in 1998.[35]

Wealth also brings other benefits to the institution. If you walk onto the campus of a leading public university and then onto the campus of a leading private university, you can see the difference. At the private institution, buildings are newer and better maintained, grounds are more richly landscaped, classrooms and dorms and public areas are cleaner and brighter, faculty offices are better furnished, and labo-ratories more lavishly appointed. But then there are a lot of import-ant differences that you can't see, such as the amount of information technology support, faculty travel budgets, graduate student stipends, career services, and recreational facilities. This can even extend to student costs. Even though the sticker price for student tuition is much higher at a top private university—in 2014, for example, almost $50,000 at Northwestern versus about $14,000 at Michigan (for state residents)—endowment funds at the top private schools allow them to heavily discount this price, so that low- and middle-income fam-ilies often find the private option less expensive. Below the top tier, private schools are more likely to offer merit scholarships to attract high-performing students who can afford to pay the full freight. In all these ways, wealth helps the private university become both more attractive and selective in recruiting the kinds of faculty and students that in turn make it look good.

Finally, wealth also draws more wealth. A private university's high academic standing, obtained in part through its deep pockets, means that families are willing to pay more money to send their children there, which then brings in more tuition. In the stratified market of American higher education, high tuition is a signal of high quality. For a private institution to charge significantly less that its peers is to suggest that it is not at the same academic level.[36] So it pays to have a sticker price that is in line with the institutions you want seen as your peers, and then discount heavily.

You see the same pattern with research grants and donations. Re-search funding agencies like to invest in institutions with the kind of talent and resources that suggest they will be able to complete a grant successfully. So it pays to give grants to universities that have long been the largest grant getters. Likewise with donors. Philanthropists like to invest in winners, where they think they will be able to see posi-tive results from their donations. Just as tuition is a signal of quality, so is endowment. So colleges that need donations the most get the least, and the rich get richer. Not only are the wealthy private schools seen as a low-risk, high-return investment, they also provide the donor with the glow of association with an institution of high prestige. A donor may have accumulated a lot of wealth in his or her lifetime, but the connection with a top private university—signaled by your name on a building or on a professorial chair—provides the kind of cultural capital that only such a great university can bestow.

So wealth provides private universities with a lot of advantages. But keep in mind that almost no private college can survive without government subsidies, direct and indirect. The only exceptions are a tiny number of institutions, such as Hillsdale College, that refuse to submit to any governmental restrictions on their operations. Private research universities are particularly dependent on these funds. And it's also important to recognize that gifts to universities would be sharply reduced without the federal tax deduction, which in the highest bracket in 2014 (39.6 percent) allows someone to donate $1 million dollars at a net cost of $604,000 because of a federal tax subsidy of $396,000. And once the money enters the university endowment, its value multiplies free of taxation. In addition, the primary source of the research grants, on which all research universities depend so heavily, is the federal government—which, in its generosity, also allows universities to own and market the patents on innovations developed with federal money. And then, of course, there is the money the federal government provides for the grants and loans that allow students to enroll in these universities.

TRADITION

One reason that private universities are so wealthy is that they are so old. It pays to be first out of the gate. Long before there was a robust public sector in American higher education, there was a lean and hungry private sector. The early private college was neither rich nor secure, but it was well established in the early nineteenth century before states started to launch public institutions in significant numbers; and it was prohibitively dominant at the start of the twentieth century, when annual funding finally made the public university secure in its own existence. As we saw, it wasn't until the middle of the twentieth century that public institutions finally achieved a firm majority of student enrollments.

In the Northeast, where private colleges settled in during the colonial era, well before the start of a public sector, they have long had and continue to have a dominant position. As a result, public universities were slow in developing in that part of the country, often not emerging until spurred to do so by federal land grants. Since Harvard was there first, in 1636, there was no need for a University of Massachusetts until a land grant brought it into existence 227 years later in 1863. Because of Yale (1718), the University of Connecticut didn't emerge until 1881. And by the time states in the area started establishing public universities, they often found that the name was already taken. In New Jersey, the state university didn't appear until 1864, when an old colonial college—originally Queens College (1766), later renamed Rutgers College (1825) after a donor—won the federal land grant over Princeton (established in 1746). But since Princeton's official name was the College of New Jersey, the new public institution had to call itself, awkwardly, Rutgers, the State University of New Jersey. The University of Pennsylvania won its charter in 1755, so when the state won a land grant in 1855 it had to call the new institution Pennsylvania State College (awarded the university label a century later).

The most extreme case of a late bloomer is New York, which set up state normal schools and agricultural colleges in the nineteenth century but didn't establish a state university system until 1948. One problem was Columbia, founded almost 200 years earlier in 1754 (originally called King's College, but this turned out to be an embarrassing name after the revolution)—which made a public university seem like an afterthought. And by the time the latter came into existence, the name New York University was already taken by a private institution (founded back in 1831); so the new system had to adopt the less than mellifluous title, State University of New York (SUNY). Under these circumstances, it is not surprising that the public universities in the Northeast had trouble establishing themselves as serious research universities. Nor is it surprising that the most distinguished American public universities tend to be located in the West (Berkeley,

UCLA) and Midwest (Michigan, Wisconsin), where they did not have to compete with entrenched private institutions.

The advantages that come from age are substantial. If you're there first, you have a chance to lock up the resources that matter, making it extremely difficult for a newcomer to break in. One such resource is talent. You get the pick of the best scholars to join your faculty, and the late arrival has to sort through your rejects. Even if the latter can get going with a second-tier faculty, it's hard to see how it manages to catch up. The professors in a new college want to work their way into an old college as soon as possible in order to show that they really belong in the top tier. Every scholar wants the best letterhead, and that's usually the one whose watermark shows the oldest founding date.

The same dynamic occurs with students. The established college is the name brand, and you want the benefits that come from association with that brand. This is the what-school-did-you-go-to problem. Example 1: John Bunting was a working-class guy who rose to the presidency of a large bank in Philadelphia in the 1970s. He used to joke that he went to "Temple O." When he would tell people he went to Philadelphia's Temple University (instead of the more prestigious Penn), they would say, "Oh." Example 2: All nine of the Supreme Court justices in 2015 went to Yale or Harvard law schools; none ever attended a public university as undergrad or grad. The last U.S. president to have any degree from a public institution was Jimmy Carter (the Naval Academy). In fact, if you don't count military academies, only three presidents since 1850 had any degrees from a public institution (Benjamin Harrison, Gerald Ford, and Lyndon Johnson). So for anyone who sees college as a way to get ahead or stay ahead in social position—and these are the two primary reasons that people go to college—the advantage of going to the oldest and (what's usually the same) most prestigious institution are clear.

Another advantage that comes from age is that the earliest college in a region gets itself deeply embedded in the local class structure. As the only game in town, the college has a lock on educating the leading families. Harvard has been graduating the children of the social, economic, and political elite of Boston for 375 years. What chance does the University of Massachusetts have to compete with that? And this is not just or even especially a matter of attracting the smartest students; it's a matter of developing associations with wealth, position, and power. In 1961, Harvard's dean of admissions, Wilbur J. Bender, wrote an article in the *Harvard Alumni Bulletin* with the intriguing title, "The Top-One-Percent Policy: A Hard Look at the Dangers of an Academically Elite Harvard."[37] His argument was simple. Harvard could admit only the most academically talented students if it chose, but that would be a mistake. Instead, it needed a balance between admitting the socially elite and the academically elite. The former would become leaders, who would reinforce Harvard's relationship with power and its broader social and cultural influence; the latter would only become "scholars, scientists, teachers." He pointed out that neither Franklin nor Theodore Roosevelt was a very good student, but excluding them would not have helped "Harvard's influence on the world." He continues:

> Then, there is the crude, practical question of the effect of a top-one percent policy on the future financing of Harvard. Harvard is a great university partly at least because it is rich, although it is rich partly because it is great. Harvard's wealth has come out of its special mixture of gentlemen and scholars, with the gentlemen, for whatever reason, giving of their substance to support the scholars. The eighty-two plus million raised for the Program for Harvard College did not come to any significant degree from the scholars, the *summas*, and the Phi Beta Kappas.[38]

This association with the socially elite not only strengthens Harvard's wealth and influence; it also helps attract students. Attending it not only gives you a degree certifying your intellectual merit; it also gives you an association with the larger network of power. This makes Harvard doubly attractive, since it provides you with both cultural capital and social capital, the right skills and the right connections. Of course, this association with the right people that the oldest private universities developed earlier than anyone else gave them privileged access to wealthy donors. So their age is also a big factor in their sub-sequent affluence.

At the core of the old and wealthy group of private universities are the institutions in the Ivy League. Seven of these eight colleges (all except Cornell) were founded in the colonial period. (The only other extant colonial colleges are Rutgers and William and Mary.) Although the colleges are old, the Ivy label is relatively new. The first published references to the Ivy League appeared in sports pages in the 1930s, and the athletic league itself wasn't formally established until 1954. This is a reminder that even the oldest American colleges are quite new compared to their European predecessors. Colleges that emerged in the eighteenth century are a big deal in the United States, but they are infants compared to places like the University of Bologna, University of Paris, and Oxford University, which emerged in the eleventh and twelfth centuries.

The reference to ivy comes from traditions invented in the late nineteenth century, when the higher education market was becoming crowded with competitors and the old colleges started to emphasize their age as a source of distinction. Graduating classes started planting ivy as part of a campaign to reproduce the ivy-covered walls of the venerable European universities. This was the period when American higher education generated many other instant traditions. Before the 1890s, college architecture in the United States had been eclectic and undistinguished. But suddenly colleges felt compelled to adopt the pointed arches of the Gothic style and build quadrangles in imitation of the medieval cloister.

The competition was coming not just from the surge of public in-stitutions but more saliently from the array of new private universities that were founded during this time near the end of the nineteenth century. These new privates had two big advantages that struck fear into the hearts of administrators of the Ivies and other old privates. One is that they emerged de novo in the form of the new research university model, which the old schools were only gradually adopting. This potentially made the earlier colleges look not so much old as old-fashioned. The other is that, instead of emerging organically over time and under difficult financial conditions as the Ivies did, they arose as fully formed instant universities with massive endowments from Gilded Age benefactors. The wealth of philanthropists like Hopkins, Vanderbilt, Rockefeller (Chicago), Duke, and Stanford promised to give the Ivy universities a run for their much-less-substantial money. This is also the time when the Ivies, following the lead of Charles W. Eliot of Harvard, started to work on developing substantial endowments that would help them compete with the newcomers.

The Mingling of Public and Private in the American System of Higher Education

Peculiar traits of private universities in the United States have given them substantial advantages over public universities, but American public universities have adopted a number of these traits, which in turn have given them substantial advantages over public universities elsewhere in the world. As a result, the American university across both sectors has important shared characteristics. Clark Kerr, the former chancellor of Berkeley and president of the University of California in the 1960s and 1970s, defined it this way: "The modern American university . . . is not Oxford nor is it Berlin; it is a new type of institution in the world. As a new type of institution, it is not really private and it is not really public; it is neither entirely of the world nor entirely apart from it. It is unique."[39]

Private universities in the United States are "not really private" in the usual sense of the word, because they are established as not-for-profit enterprises organized to serve the public interest. This distinction has become clearer in recent years as a for-profit sector of higher education has emerged as a major player. The newcomers are organizations for providing educational services to student clients in the interest of enhancing shareholder value. They may generate benefits for students and for society, but if so, these would be unintended side effects of the main mission, which is to produce a high financial return on investment. Like other universities, they need to compete effectively to attract and retain tuition-paying students. But not-for-profit universities subsidize students by redistributing tuition dollars from wealthy to poor students and by drawing on endowment income. For example, the sticker price for Stanford undergraduate tuition in 2014 was about $44,000, but families with incomes under $125,000 paid nothing. In 2015, *Money* magazine selected Stanford as the college having the best value for students measured by cost over benefit.[40]

For-profit institutions provide no such subsidies. Instead, they rely on customers who qualify for federal grants and loans and are willing to apply these funds toward the full tuition. The demographics of the for-profit student pool are such that relatively few students are able to pay tuition out of their own resources. Only 21 percent come from the top half of the income distribution; fully 57 percent come from the bottom quartile—compared to 40 percent of community college students and about a quarter of public and private four-year colleges.[41] So in the absence of federal funds, the for-profits would be out of business—which is what happened in 2015 to one large chain:

> Corinthian Colleges, a for-profit college company that was formerly a Wall Street favorite, filed Monday for Chapter 11 bankruptcy, listing $143 million in debt and less than $20 million in assets. Based in Santa Ana, Calif., Corinthian was once one of the nation's largest for-profit college companies, enrolling more than 100,000 students at its 100 Everest, Heald and WyoTech campuses. But for the last few years, the company has faced charges of predatory recruiting and false placement and graduation rates. It went into its death spiral last year when the Department of Education suspended its access to the federal student aid it depended on, and then brokered the sale of most of its campuses.[42]

Private universities also have other characteristics that align them with the publics. Although their autonomy allows them the option of being frankly elitist, the system strongly encourages them not to do so. They can afford to have a stronger emphasis on graduate education then their public counterparts, but they can't survive and thrive without maintaining a strong undergraduate presence. Flexner's dream of a university with a pure focus on graduate programs and research has recurred from time to time, but it has never been able to gain traction in the United States. Johns Hopkins tried it briefly and quickly relented; Clark persisted longer and paid the price by falling quickly down the rankings. Chicago under Robert Maynard Hutchins toyed with the idea but never went through with it (although it did drop top-tier football). The issue is that the system's uniquely broad base of political, social, and economic support depended on institutions maintaining a balance among its three core functions: populist, elite, and practical.

A large undergraduate student body is essential to support the elite enterprise of research and graduate study. This is what justifies hiring all of those professors, what subsidizes research and graduate programs, what connects the university more closely to the larger community, and what makes even a private university feel socially accessible. Athletics, especially football and basketball, reinforce the populist appeal of what might otherwise be a remote and socially exclusive institution. The Ivies, relying on age and wealth, can manage to prosper within their own exclusive league. But other private universities mingle with public universities in diverse athletic leagues. Stanford and University of Southern California play in the Pac 12 conference along with publics such as Berkeley and Oregon. Boston College, Duke, Miami, Notre Dame, Syracuse, and Wake Forest all play in the Atlantic Coast Conference along with publics such as Florida State and North Carolina. Since private universities are smaller, they are often at a disadvantage in intercollegiate sports that thrive on a large undergraduate student body. So they are less likely to compete at the Division I level in a large-squad sport such as football, but basketball offers them better prospects (think Vanderbilt, Villanova, and Penn). Still, public and private universities act so much alike that they are surprisingly hard to tell apart. Even though I am particularly attuned to the public-private distinction, I find that I continually have to look online to find which label a particular university bears.

At the same time that private universities in the United States are not really private, public universities are not really public. Like their private counterparts, public universities depend heavily on revenues from student tuition, raise large sums of money from donations, aggressively pursue research grants, market patented products developed by faculty, and develop lucrative ties with industry. In short, they act as entrepreneurial organizations operating in a competitive higher education marketplace. And they do so because they emerged in a peculiarly American system of higher education where such behavior was a necessity. Private colleges arose first in the American setting because the state was too poor to supply public funds and a market economy filled this void. People started colleges in order to enhance local land values in a setting where land was plentiful and buyers had lots of options and in order to promote the faith in a setting where religious denominations were plentiful and congregants had lots of options. By the time states started establishing public colleges, the system was already firmly in place. The new public institutions did not change the system's DNA because the same conditions persisted. States did not have enough money to provide full support for the new public colleges, and they didn't feel the need to do so because the pattern was already established that colleges were capable of fending for themselves.

Public universities in the United States have grown up in a market-based system of higher education that tutored them on strategies for operating effectively under competitive market conditions. They learned their lessons well. In the process, they adopted in somewhat weaker form, the traits that have given the privates their enormous strength: autonomy, affluence, and tradition. Of these, by far the most important has been autonomy.

American private universities have considerably more autonomy than public universities, but American public universities in turn have considerably more autonomy than their counterparts in other countries. In most countries, universities are subject to a government ministry and their administrators and professors are civil servants. While they enjoy some traditional autonomy in academic matters, their funding and salaries and enrollments are determined by the government. Public universities in the United States enjoy more latitude than

this, and the best universities have the most autonomy. Consider this
finding from a study examining the relationship between university
autonomy and productivity: "For the U.S., we show that states' public
universities differ considerably in their autonomy and the degree to
which they face local competition from private universities. We find
that universities' output is higher in the states in which they are more
autonomous and face more competition."[43] The authors measure a
university's output by its rank in the Shanghai global university index,
which includes such factors as academic citations and faculty awards.
They found a strong correlation between autonomy and rank. State
universities in Washington, Colorado, Hawaii, Delaware, California,
Maryland, Wisconsin, Minnesota, and Michigan had high rankings
and high autonomy. Universities in Arkansas, South Carolina, Loui-
siana, Kansas, Idaho, South Dakota, and Wyoming were low in both
dimensions.[44]

There are three degrees of autonomy that public universities have in
the United States. The strongest is constitutional autonomy, in which
language in the constitution buffers the university from interference
by the governor and legislature. Michigan, Minnesota, California, and
Colorado all enjoy this status. Listen to the protective language of
the Michigan constitution: "The power of the institutions of higher
education provided in this constitution to supervise their respective
institutions and control and direct the expenditures of the institutions'
funds shall not be limited to this section."[45] In Michigan, the three top
state universities (Michigan, Michigan State, and Wayne State) have
boards of trustees that are elected statewide; for other universities,
mostly former teachers colleges, the governor appoints the board. In
California in the 1870s, the constitution created the University of California board of regents as a public trust, which alone has the authority
to open campuses, develop programs, and set admissions standards. It
is no coincidence that University of California, Berkeley, and University of Michigan consistently rank as the two best public universities
in the United States. And in 2014 they were ranked the fourth and
seventeenth best universities of all types in the world. Remarkably,
four of the ten UC campuses ranked among the top twenty universi-

ties in the world, six in the top fifty. Two other public universities with constitutional autonomy, Minnesota and Colorado, in turn ranked thirtieth and thirty-fourth, respectively.[46]

A second tier of autonomy grants public universities the status of public corporations, which limits the degree of interference that legislatures can initiate. The Universities of Wisconsin, Illinois, Maryland, and Hawaii all have this status. It seems to pay off. In world rankings, Wisconsin comes in at twenty-four, Illinois at twenty-eight, and Maryland at forty-three.

The lowest tier of autonomy is statutory. This means that the legislature has established the university's autonomy by statute, but it has the ability to change this at any time. Universities in this situation are less able to control their own fate, but they are partially buffered by a tradition of leaving universities relatively free of interference. And they still reap some benefits. Three such universities—Washington, North Carolina, and Texas—rank in the top forty in the world. By comparison, of all the universities in continental Europe—which operate more as government agencies than as independent enterprises—only three rank in the top forty.[47]

American public universities not only have some of the autonomy of their private counterparts, but they also have some of the wealth. Of the top fifty college endowments, only thirteen belong to individual public universities. But this wealth would be the envy of European universities. By far the richest university in Europe is Cambridge, with an endowment of $8.1 billion, but it is topped by University of Michigan, which, although 700 years younger, has an endowment of $9.7 billion. The richest university on the continent is Zurich, with an endowment of $1.1 billion. By comparison, the lowest-ranking U.S. public university in the top fifty by endowment is Georgia Tech with $1.9 billion. So the publics only look poor when compared with Harvard. Compared with the rest of the world, they are wealthy indeed. And some of the state systems are wealthier still. The University of Texas system has $25.4 billion; Texas A&M system has $11.1 billion; and the University of California system has $7.3 billion. In 2013 alone, the UC system raised $1.6 billion from private donors.[48]

Public universities in the last thirty years have needed money from endowments and from donations in order to replace state funding, which is paying for a steadily declining share of their costs. But because of their relative autonomy, these institutions have other ways of raising funds. Pursuing research grants helps, since these pay for overhead, pick up part of the cost of faculty salaries, and subsidize a large share of the support for doctoral students. But a key fund-raising strategy relies on that old standby of the nineteenth-century college business model, student tuition. Having the ability to set the fees you charge students is an important component of university autonomy. And as we will see in more detail in the following chapter, as state appropriations declined in the late twentieth century, public universities steadily raised tuition. They did this in two ways—by raising the tuition rate for in-state students and by increasing the number of out-of-state students, who pay a tuition rate that is typically two times or even three times as high. In the complex politics of higher education in the United States, this creates a chronic source of tension between public universities and legislatures. Universities want the money that comes from higher tuition and more out-of-state students, and legislators want to keep costs low and access high for local residents. If the university has substantial autonomy, it can use the leverage of tuition and access to bargain with the legislature for funding: give us more funding and we will hold down tuition and admit more locals; otherwise, we'll have no choice but to proceed with plan B. In contrast, public universities with less autonomy may find themselves stuck both with less funding and with limits on tuition and on nonresident enrollments.

In addition to autonomy and wealth, public universities have borrowed one other implement from the private university toolkit: tradition. As we have seen, the American system of higher education has always pursued expansion by creating new lower-level institutions to take the influx of students instead of increasing the size of existing institutions. Each time they did so, the older colleges sought to buffer themselves from the newcomers by emphasizing the distinctions between institutional types. So the flagship state universities in the mid-nineteenth century stressed their differences from the new land-grant colleges, which in the early twentieth century in turn stressed their differences from the teachers colleges, which by midcentury in turn sought to mark themselves off from community colleges. The theme is constant: older is better. Older institutions are academically superior and more selective and more prestigious. Just as the Ivies lorded it over the newer private colleges, each of the tiers of the public system has lorded it over the tier below. In state after state, you could see this dynamic play itself out. For example, the University of Michigan had long resisted any attempt to give the label university to any other public institutions in the state. But when the legislature finally agreed in the 1950s to turn the land-grant school, Michigan State College, into a university, the University of Michigan immediately lobbied hard and successfully to flood the market by having all of the teachers colleges also elevated to university status. The message is clear. There's really only one University of Michigan; all the rest are pretenders.[49]

There is also one other way in which private universities have exerted a major impact on public universities: they supply a disproportionate share of their faculty. Drawing on a 1966 study, Edward Shils makes this point: "The eminence of the public universities is in part a result of the accomplishment of the private universities. The members of the five most distinguished departments in each of the fields surveyed by Dr. Alan Cartter were trained predominantly in private universities. Of 372 members of the departments of history, classics, English, French, German, linguistics, music, philosophy, Russian, and Spanish in these universities, 82 percent had their most advanced degree from private universities."[50]

I have been unable to find more recent systematic data on American professors by source of degree, so I tried looking at four institutions from two different tiers of the California system of public higher education. I looked at the tenure-track faculty members in two departments, history and psychology. Berkeley and UCLA are the top institutions in the University of California system and two of the great research universities in the world. San José State and California State University, Los Angeles, are both members of the teaching-intensive California State University system, where research is secondary and

TABLE 1. Sources of PhDs of tenured and tenure-track faculty, by department

	Private University		Public University		Foreign University		Internal Hires	
	%	n	%	n	%	n	%	n
Berkeley:								
History	66	35	25	13	9	5	15	8
Psychology	59	22	27	10	14	5	3	1
UCLA:								
History	58	42	27	20	15	11	12	9
Psychology	37	32	57	50	6	5	17	15
SJSU:								
History	46	5	54	6	0	0	0	0
Psychology	4	1	92	22	4	1	0	0
CSULA:								
History	24	5	76	16	0	0	0	0
Psychology	39	7	61	11	0	0	0	0

Note. I am grateful to Ethan Ris for compiling the data for this table.
Sources. University departmental websites, accessed June 2015. Internal hires represent faculty members who earned their degrees at their institution of employment and are thus a subset of the "Public University" group.

no PhDs are offered. The results for faculty listed on university websites in the spring of 2015 are presented in table 1.

If we just look at the faculty with American PhDs, we find a striking pattern. In the four departments at the two research universities, 58 percent of the faculty had degrees from private universities—this in spite of the fact that three of the departments showed a tendency to hire their own graduates. At the two comprehensive universities, 25 percent of the faculty had private degrees. The result shouldn't be that surprising, since we previously established that top-ranked departments provide the lion's share of faculty at all departments; recall that in sociology, the top five departments provided one-third of all faculty and the top twenty provided two-thirds.[51] And, as we have also seen, private universities occupy disproportionate space in the top ranks. In history, four of the top five departments are private; in psychology it is two of the top five.[52] Even so, however, it is stunning to see the extent to which private university graduates have colonized public universities. A sizable majority of faculty in these departments at the public research universities had private degrees, along with a quarter of faculty in comprehensive universities. To me it's particularly interesting to see the private impact on the lowest tier of the four-year public system, which are effectively open-access institutions. In 2014,

CSU admitted 72 percent of the nearly 210,000 students applying to be first-time freshmen.[53] Even here, the private universities are exerting a significant influence.

What we find in this analysis is that there is a paradox in the relationship between public and private institutions of higher education in the United States. Private universities have enormous advantages over public universities, in particular, selectivity, autonomy, wealth, and age. In this sense, then, harkening back to the discussion in the previous chapter, the private sector seems to be the zone of advantage in the system while the public sector is the zone of access. The private universities exclude most applicants and provide the privileged few with the extraordinary social benefits of a highly prestigious degree. But we have also seen that things are not this simple. The majority of private colleges are neither very distinguished nor very selective. It's the ones at the top that garner all the best students and faculty and the most donations and Nobel prizes.

And the public system contains its own hierarchy. For graduates of the University of Michigan, the chances of getting ahead or staying ahead are high; the chances decline but remain reasonably high for graduates of Michigan State University, decline further for graduates of Central Michigan University, and start looking bleaker for graduates of Lansing Community College. If you examine this public hierarchy closely, you see that the institutions in each tier have advantages over those in the tier below that parallel the advantages private universities have over public universities. The institutions in each tier of the public system are more selective, more autonomous, wealthier, and older than those in the tier below.

In addition, the relationship between private and public is not a simple case of master and servant; it's more like master and apprentice. The private colleges established the structure of the American system of higher education before there were any public colleges, and the public institutions have learned how to play the game designed by their predecessors. They have learned how to survive with uncertain public funding, to preserve their autonomy, and to compete effectively in a glutted market, pursuing opportunities as they appear on the horizon and always seeking to satisfy the all-powerful consumer. This is especially apparent in the top tier of the system occupied by public research universities. As a result, these institutions have been able to be highly successful players in their own right in the world market of higher education. The Shanghai rankings tell both parts of this story. Of the top forty universities in the world in 2014, American private universities accounted for sixteen, which is an extraordinary showing. But American public universities accounted for twelve of the top forty, which itself is extraordinary, since universities in the top forty from all of the rest of the countries in the world also amounted to twelve.[54] Private universities dominate in the American system, but by sharing their secrets with the public sector they have enabled public universities to occupy a dauntingly strong position in global higher education.

7

LEARNING TO LOVE THE BOMB

*America's Brief Cold War Fling with
the University as a Public Good*

American higher education rose to fame and fortune during the Cold War, when both student enrollments and funded research shot upward. Prior to the Second World War, the federal government showed little interest in universities and provided little support. The war spurred a large investment in defense-based scientific research in universities for reasons of both efficiency and necessity: universities had the researchers and infrastructure in place and the government needed to gear up quickly. With the emergence of the Cold War in 1947, the relationship continued, and federal investment expanded exponentially. Unlike a hot war, the Cold War offered a long time line for global competition between communism and democracy, which meant institutionalizing the wartime model of federally funded research and building a set of structures for continuing investment in knowledge whose military value was unquestioned. At the same time, the communist challenge provided a strong rationale for sending a large number of students to college. These increased enrollments would educate the skilled workers needed by the Cold War economy, produce informed citizens to combat the Soviet menace, and demonstrate to the world the broad social opportunities available in a liberal democracy. The result of this enormous public investment in higher education has become known as the golden age of the American university.

Of course, as is so often the case with a golden age, it didn't last.

The good times continued for about thirty years and then began to go bad. The decline was triggered by the combination of a decline in the perceived Soviet threat and a taxpayer revolt against high public spending; both trends came to a head with the fall of the Berlin Wall in 1989. With no money and no enemy, the Cold War university fell as quickly as it arose.

In this chapter I try to make sense of this short-lived institution. But I want to avoid the note of nostalgia that pervades many current academic accounts, in which professors and administrators grieve for the good old days of the midcentury university and spin fantasies of recapturing them. Barring another national crisis of the same dimension, it just won't happen. Instead of seeing the Cold War university as the norm that we need to return to, I suggest that it's the exception. What we're experiencing now in American higher education is, in many ways, a regression to the mean.

My central theme is this: over the long haul, Americans have understood higher education as a distinctly private good. The period from 1940 to 1970 was the one time in our history when the university became a public good. And now we are back to the place we have always been, where the university's primary role is to provide individual consumers a chance to gain social access and social advantage. Since students are the primary beneficiaries, then they should also foot the bill; so state subsidies are harder to justify.

The Long History of U.S. Higher Ed as a Private Good

As we saw in chapters 2 and 3, the American system of higher education is deeply rooted in markets rather than politics. It had to make its own way without the guiding hand and generous purse of governmental or religious sponsors. Its earliest prototype was the nineteenth-century liberal arts college, with a state charter and religious affiliation but largely left to its own devices to survive in an environment crowded with competitors. The primary interests it served were private. For religious denominations, it established a beachhead in the territories of the advancing frontier in order to maintain their position in relation to competitor sects. And for towns on the frontier, it provided a way to boost cultural standing, attract settlers, and raise property values. Even when states got into the business of establishing colleges under their own control and finance, they often did so in order to announce themselves as something more than an outpost on the frontier since they now had their own real university.

Then came another private interest in the college, from the student-consumer. After 1880, the primary benefits of the system went to the students who enrolled. For them, it became the central way to gain entry to the relatively secure confines of salaried work in management and the professions. For middle-class families, college in this period emerged as the main mechanism for transmitting social advantage from parents to children, and for others, it became the object of aspiration as the place to get access to the middle class. State governments put increasing amounts of money into support for public higher education, less because of the public benefits it would produce than because voters demanded increasing access to this very attractive private good.

Of course, this growth in higher education, even though driven by the private interests of consumers, also produced broad public benefits, such as greater economic productivity and a rising standard of living. In this sense, U.S. higher ed did and does serve as a public good, whose largesse accrues to the entire community and not just the ones who graduate from college. But my point is that consumer demand for private benefit was the primary factor driving the expansion of the system.

So spurred by student desire to get ahead and stay ahead, college enrollments started growing quickly around 1880.

Year	Total College Enrollments
1879	116,000
1889	157,000
1899	238,000
1909	355,000
1919	598,000
1929	1,104,000
1939	1,494,000[1]

This was a rate of increase of more than 50 percent a decade—not as fast as the increases that would come at midcentury, but still impressive. During this same sixty-year period, total college enrollment as a proportion of the population eighteen to twenty-four years old rose from 1.6 percent to 9.1 percent. Enrollments were growing more at public colleges than private colleges, but only by a small margin. And the increases occurred across all levels of the system, including the top public research universities, but the largest share of enrollments flowed into the newer institutions at the bottom of the system: the state colleges that were emerging from normal schools, urban commuter colleges (mostly private), and an array of public and private junior colleges that offered two-year vocational programs.

For the purposes of this chapter, the key point is this: the American system of colleges and universities that emerged in the nineteenth century and continued until the Second World War was a market-driven structure that construed higher education as a private good. The state was too weak and too poor to provide strong support for higher education, and there was no obvious state interest that argued for doing so. Until the decade before the war, most student enrollments were in the private sector, and the majority of institutions in the system were private (and remain so today).[2]

The Rise of the Cold War University

And then came the Second World War. There is no need here to recount the devastation it brought about or the nightmarish residue it left. But it's worth keeping in mind the peculiar fact that this conflict is remembered fondly by Americans, who often refer to it as the Good War.[3] The war cost a lot of American lives and money, but it also brought a lot of benefits. It didn't hurt, of course, to be on the winning side and to have all the fighting take place on foreign soil. And part of the positive feeling associated with the war comes from the way it thrust the country into a new role as the dominant world power. But perhaps even more, the warm feeling arises from the memory of this as a time when the country came together around a common cause.

For citizens of the United States—the most liberal of liberal democracies, where private liberty is much more highly valued than public loyalty—it was a novel and exciting feeling to rally around the federal government. Usually viewed with suspicion as a threat to the rights of individuals and a drain on private wealth, the American government in the 1940s took on the mantle of good in the fight against evil. Its public image became the resolute face of Uncle Sam as a famous recruiting poster, saying "I want *you*."

One consequence of the war was a sharp increase in the size of the U.S. government. The historically small federal state had started to grow substantially in the 1930s as a result of the New Deal effort to spend the country out of a decade-long economic depression, a time when the budget doubled. But the war raised the level of federal spending by a factor of seven, from $1,000 to $7,000 per capita. After the war, the level dropped back to $2,000, and then the onset of the Cold War sent federal spending into a sharp, and this time sustained, increase—reaching $3,000 in the 1950s, $4,000 in the 1960s, and regaining the previous high of $7,000 in the 1980s, during the last days of the Soviet Union.[4]

If, for Americans in general, the Second World War carries warm associations, for people in higher education it marks the beginning of the Best of Times—a short but intense period of generous public funding and rapid expansion. Initially, of course, the war brought trouble, since it sent most prospective college students into the military. Colleges quickly adapted by repurposing their facilities for military training and other war-related activities. But the real long-term benefits came when the federal government decided to draw higher education more centrally into the war effort—first, as the central site for military research and development, and second, as the place to send veterans when the war was over. Let me say a little about each.

In the first half of the twentieth century, university researchers had to rummage around looking for funding, forced to rely on a mix of foundations, corporations, and private donors. The federal government saw little benefit in employing their services. In a particularly striking case at the start of First World War, the professional association of academic chemists offered its help to the War Department, which declined "on the grounds that it already had a chemist in its employ."[5] The existing model was for government to maintain its own modest research facilities instead of relying on the university.

The scale of the next war changed all this. At the very start, a former engineering dean from MIT, Vannevar Bush, took charge of mobilizing university scientists behind the war effort as head of the Office of Scientific Research and Development. The model he established for managing the relationship between government and researchers set the pattern for university research that still exists in the United States today. Instead of setting up government centers, the idea was to farm out research to universities: issue a request for proposals to meet a particular research need, award the grant to the academic researchers who seemed best equipped to meet this need, and pay 50 percent or more overhead to the university for the facilities that researchers would use.

This method drew on the expertise and facilities that already existed at research universities, which both saved the government from having to maintain a costly permanent research operation and gave it the flexibility to draw on the right people for particular projects and then change direction at will. For universities, it provided a large source of funds, which enhanced their research reputations, helped them expand faculty, and paid for infrastructure. It was a win-win situation. It also established the entrepreneurial model of the university researcher in perpetual search for grant money. And for the first time in the history of American higher education, the university was being considered primarily a public good, whose research capacity could serve the national interest by helping to win a war.

If universities could meet one national need during the war by providing military research, they could meet another national need after the war by enrolling veterans. The GI Bill of Rights, passed by Congress in 1944, was designed to pay off a debt and resolve a manpower problem. Its official name, the Servicemen's Readjustment Act of 1944, reflects both aims. By the end of the war there were fifteen million men and women who had served in the military, and they clearly deserved a reward for their years of service to the country. The bill offered them the opportunity to continue their education at federal expense, which included attending the college of their choice.

This opportunity also offered another public benefit, since it responded to deep concern about the ability of the economy to absorb this flood of veterans. The country had been sliding back into depression at the start of the war, and the fear was that massive unemployment at war's end was a real possibility. The strategy worked. Under the GI Bill, about two million veterans eventually attended some form of college. By 1948, when veteran enrollment peaked, American colleges and universities had one million more students than ten years earlier.[6] This was another win-win situation. The state rewarded national service, headed off mass unemployment, and produced a pile of human capital for future growth. Higher education got a flood of students with full scholarships. The worry, of course, was what was going to happen when the wartime research contracts ended and the veterans graduated.

That's where the Cold War came in to save the day. And the timing was perfect. The first major action of the new conflict—the Berlin Blockade—came in 1948, the same year that veteran enrollments at American colleges reached their peak. If the Second World War was good for American higher education, the Cold War was a bonanza. The hot war meant boom and bust—providing a short surge of money and students followed by a sharp decline. But the Cold War was a prolonged effort to contain communism. It was more sustainable because actual combat was limited and often carried out by proxies. For universities, this was a gift that, for thirty years, kept on giving. The military threat was massive in scale—nothing less than the threat of nuclear annihilation. And supplementing it was an ideological challenge—the competition between two social and political systems for hearts and minds.

As a result, the government needed top universities to provide it with massive amounts of scientific research that would support the military effort. And it also needed all levels of the higher education system to educate the large numbers of citizens required to deal with the ideological menace. We needed to produce the scientists and engineers who would allow us to compete with Soviet technology. We needed to provide high-level human capital in order to promote economic growth and demonstrate the economic superiority of capitalism over communism. And we needed to provide educational opportunity for our own racial minorities and lower classes in order to show that our system is not only effective but also fair and equitable. This would be a powerful weapon in the effort to win over the Third World with the attractions of the American way. The Cold War American government treated the higher education system as a highly valuable public good, which would make a large contribution to the national interest, and the system was pleased to be the object of so much federal investment.[7]

On the research side, the impact of the Cold War on American universities was dramatic. The best way to measure this is by examining patterns of federal research and development spending over the years, which traces the ebb and flow of national threats across the last sixty years. Funding rose slowly from $13 billion in 1953 (in constant 2014 dollars) until the Sputnik crisis (after the Soviets succeeded in placing the first satellite in earth orbit), when funding jumped to $40 billion in 1959 and rose rapidly to a peak of $88 billion in 1967. Then the amount backed off to $66 billion in 1975, climbing to a new peak of $104 billion in 1990 just before the collapse of the Soviet Union and then began to drop off. It started growing again in 2002 after the attack on the Twin Towers, reaching an all-time high of $151 billion in 2010, and has been declining ever since.[8]

Initially, defense funding accounted for 85 percent of federal research funding, gradually falling back to a little over half in 1967, as nondefense funding increased, but remaining in a solid majority position up until the present. For most of the period after 1957, however, the largest element in nondefense spending was research on space technology, which arose directly from the Soviet Sputnik threat. If you combine defense and space appropriations, this accounts for about three-quarters of federal research funding until 1990. Defense research closely tracked perceived threats in the international environment, dropping by 20 percent after 1989 and then making a comeback in 2001. Overall, federal funding during the Cold War for research of all types grew in constant dollars from $13 billion in 1953 to $104 in 1990, an increase of 700 percent. These were good times for university researchers.[9]

At the same time that research funding was growing rapidly, so were college enrollments. The number of students in American higher education grew from 2.4 million in 1949 to 3.6 million in 1959. But then came the 1960s, when enrollments more than doubled, reaching eight million in 1969. The number hit 11.6 million in 1979 and then growth began to slow down—creeping up to 13.5 million in 1989 and leveling off at around fourteen million in the 1990s.[10] During the thirty years between 1949 and 1979, enrollments increased by more than nine million students, a growth of almost 400 percent. And the bulk of the enrollment increases in the last two decades have been in part-time students and at two-year colleges. Among four-year institutions, the primary growth has occurred not at private or flagship public universities but at regional state universities, the former normal schools. The Cold War was not just good for research universities; it was also great for institutions of higher education all the way down the status ladder.

In part we can understand this radical growth in college enrollments as an extension of the long-term surge in consumer demand for American higher education as a private good. Recall that enrollments started accelerating late in the nineteenth century, when college attendance started to provide an edge in gaining middle-class jobs. This meant that attending college gave middle-class families a way to pass on social advantage while attending high school gave working-class families a way to gain social opportunity. But by 1940, high school enrollments had become universal. So for working-class families, the new zone of social opportunity became higher education. This increase in consumer demand provided a market-based explanation for at least part of the flood of postwar enrollments.

At the same time, however, the Cold War provided a strong public rationale for broadening access to college. In 1946, President Harry

Truman appointed a commission to provide a plan for expanding access to higher education, which was the first time in American history that a president sought advice about education at any level. The result was a six-volume report with the title *Higher Education for American Democracy*. It's no coincidence that the report was issued in 1947, the starting point of the Cold War. The authors framed the report around the new threat of atomic war, arguing that "it is essential today that education come decisively to grips with the worldwide crisis of mankind."[11] What they proposed as a public response to the crisis was a dramatic increase in access to higher education.

> The American people should set as their ultimate goal an educational system in which at no level—high school, college, graduate school, or professional school—will a qualified individual in any part of the country encounter an insuperable economic barrier to the attainment of the kind of education suited to his aptitudes and interests. This means that we shall aim at making higher education equally available to all young people, as we now do education in the elementary and high schools, to the extent that their capacity warrants a further social investment in their training.[12]

Tellingly, the report devotes a lot of space to exploring the existing barriers to educational opportunity posed by class and race—exactly the kinds of issues that were making liberal democracies look bad in light of the egalitarian promise of communism.

Decline of the System's Public Mission

So in the mid-twentieth century, Americans went through an intense but brief infatuation with higher education as a public good. Somehow college was going to help save us from the communist menace and the looming threat of nuclear war. Like the Second World War, the Cold War brought together a notoriously individualistic population around the common goal of national survival and the preservation of liberal democracy. It was a time when every public building had an area designated as a bomb shelter. In the elementary school I attended in the 1950s, I can remember regular air raid drills. The alarm would sound and teachers would lead us downstairs to the basement, whose concrete-block walls were supposed to protect us from a nuclear blast. Although the drills did nothing to preserve life, they did serve an important social function. Like Sunday church services, these rituals drew individuals together into communities of faith where we enacted our allegiance to a higher power.

For American college professors, these were the glory years, when fear of annihilation gave us a glamorous public mission and what seemed like an endless flow of public funds and funded students. But it did not—and could not—last. Wars can bring great benefits to the home front, but then they end. The Cold War lasted longer than most, but this longevity came at the expense of intensity. By the 1970s, the United States had lived with the nuclear threat for thirty years without any sign that the worst case was going to materialize. You can only stand guard for so long before attention begins to flag and ordinary concerns start to push back to the surface. In addition, waging war is extremely expensive, draining both the public purse and public sympathy. The two Cold War conflicts that engaged American troops—Korea and Vietnam—cost a lot, stirred strong opposition, and ended badly, providing neither the idealistic glow of the Good War nor the satisfying closure of unconditional surrender by the enemy. Korea ended with a stalemate and the return to the status quo ante bellum. Vietnam ended with defeat and the humiliating image in 1975 of the last Americans being plucked off a rooftop in Saigon—which the victors then promptly renamed Ho Chi Minh City.

The Soviet menace and the nuclear threat persisted, but in a form that—after the grim experience of war in the rice paddies—seemed distant and slightly unreal. Add to this the problem that, as a tool for defeating the enemy, the radical expansion of higher education by the 1970s did not appear to be a cost-effective option. Higher ed is a very labor-intensive enterprise, in which size brings few economies of scale, and its public benefits in the war effort were hard to pin down. As the national danger came to seem more remote, the costs of higher ed became more visible and more problematic. Look around any university campus, and the primary beneficiaries of public munificence seem to be private actors—the faculty and staff who make a good living there and the students whose degrees will allow them to make a good living in the future. So about thirty years into the Cold War, the question naturally arose: Why should the public pay so much to provide cushy jobs for the first group and to subsidize the personal ambition of the second? If graduates reap major benefits from a college education, shouldn't they be paying for it rather than the beleaguered taxpayer?

The 1970s marked the beginning of the American tax revolt, and not surprisingly this revolt emerged first in the bellwether state of California. Fueled by booming defense and aerospace industries and high immigration, California had a great run in the decades after 1945. During this period, the state developed the most comprehensive system of higher education in the country. In 1960 it formalized this system with a master plan that offered every Californian the opportunity to attend college in one of three state systems. The University of California focused on research, advanced graduate programs, and educating the top high school graduates. California State University (developed mostly from former teachers colleges) focused on undergraduate programs for the second tier of high school graduates. The community college system offered the rest of the population two-year programs for vocational training and possible transfer to one of the two university systems. By 1975, there were nine campuses in the University of California, twenty-three in California State University, and ninety-six in the community college system, with a total enrollment across all systems of 1.5 million students—accounting for 14 percent of the college students in the United States.[13] Not only was the system enormous, but the California Master Plan for Higher Education declared it illegal to charge California students tuition. The biggest and best public system of higher education in the country was free.

And this was the problem. What allowed the system to grow so fast was a state fiscal regime that was quite rare in the American context—one based on high public services supported by high taxes.

After enjoying the benefits of this combination for a few years, tax-payers suddenly woke up to the realization that this approach to paying for higher education was at core, well, un-American. For a country deeply grounded in liberal democracy, the system of higher ed for all at no cost to the consumer looked a lot like socialism. So, of course, it had to go. In the mid-1970s the country's first taxpayer revolt emerged in California, culminating in a successful campaign in 1978 to pass a statewide initiative that put a limit on increases in property taxes. Other tax limitation initiatives followed.[14] As a result, the average state appropriation per student at the University of California dropped from about $3,400 (in 1960 dollars) in 1987 to $1,100 in 2010, a decline of 68 percent.[15] This quickly led to a steady increase in fees charged to students at California's colleges and universities. (Although tuition was illegal, demanding fees from students was not.) Adjusted for inflation, the annual fees for in-state undergraduates at the University of California from 1987 to 2010 rose more 250 percent to a total of more than $10,000.[16]

This pattern of tax limitations and tuition increases spread across the country. Nationwide during the same period of time, the average state appropriation per student at a four-year public college fell (in 2012 dollars) from $8,500 to $5,900, a decline of 31 percent, while average undergraduate tuition doubled, rising from $2,600 to $5,200.[17] Another way of looking at the rise and fall of government funding is to examine changes in the shares of higher education funding from different sources. The proportion of total funding for higher education from state and local governments reached a peak of 57 percent in 1977 and then dropped back to 39 percent in 2012. The proportion of funding from the federal government rose from near zero in 1952 to a peak of more than 20 percent in 1967 and then fell to 12 percent in 2012. During the same period the proportion of funding from families moved in the opposite direction, dropping from more than 50 percent in 1952 to a low of 33 percent in 1977 and then rising to 49 percent in 2012.[18]

The decline in the state share of higher education costs was most pronounced at the top public research universities, which had a wider range of income sources. By 2009, the average such institution was receiving only 25 percent of its revenue from state government.[19] An extreme case is the University of Virginia, where in 2013 the state provided less than 6 percent of the university's operating budget.[20]

While these changes were happening at the state level, the federal government was also backing away from its Cold War generosity to students in higher education. Legislation such as the National Defense Education Act (1958) and Higher Education Act (1965) had provided support for students through a roughly equal balance of grants and loans. But in 1980 the election of Ronald Reagan as president meant that the push to lower taxes would become national policy. At this point, support for students started shifting from cash support to federally guaranteed loans. The idea was that a college degree was a great investment for students, which would pay them long-term economic dividends, and as a result they should shoulder an increasing share of the cost. So over time, the proportion of average college costs paid by the maximum federal Pell Grant fell from a peak of 67 percent in 1975 to 27 percent in 2014.[21] The proportion of total student support in the form of loans was 54 percent in 1975, 67 percent in 1985, and 78 percent in 1995, and the ratio has remained at that level ever since.[22] By 1995, students were borrowing $41 billion to attend college, which grew to $89 billion in 2005.[23] At present, about 60 percent of all students accumulate college debt, most of it in the form of federal loans, and the total student debt load has passed $1 trillion.

At the same time that the federal government was cutting back on funding college students, it was also reducing funding for university research. As I mentioned earlier, federal research grants in constant dollars peaked at about $100 billion in 1990, the year after the fall of the Berlin Wall—a good marker for the end of the Cold War. At this point, defense accounted for about two-thirds of all university research funding—three-quarters if you include space research. Defense research declined by about 20 percent during the 1990s and didn't start rising again substantially until 2002, the year after the fall of the Twin Towers and the beginning of the new existential threat known as the War on Terror. Defense research reached a new peak in 2009 at a level about a third above the Cold War high, and it has been declining steadily ever since. Increases in nondefense research helped compensate for only a part of the loss of defense funds.[24]

Returning to the Norm

The American system of higher education came into existence as a distinctly private good. It arose in the nineteenth century to serve the pursuit of sectarian advantage and land speculation, and then in the twentieth century it evolved into a system for providing individual consumers a way to get ahead or stay ahead in the social hierarchy. Quite late in the game, it took the Second World War to give higher education an expansive national mission and reconstitute it as a public good. But hot wars are unsustainable for long, so in 1945 the system was sliding quickly back toward public irrelevance before it was saved by the timely arrival of the Cold War. As I have shown, the Cold War was very, very good for American system of higher education. It produced a massive increase in funding by federal and state governments, both for university research and for college student subsidies, and—more critically—it sustained this support for a period of three decades. But these golden years gradually gave way before a national wave of taxpayer fatigue and the surprising collapse of the Soviet Union. With the nation strapped for funds and with its global enemy dissolved, it no longer had the urgent need to enlist America's colleges and universities in a grand national cause. The result was a decade of declining research support and static student enrollments. In 2002, the wars in Afghanistan and Iraq brought a momentary surge in both, but these measures peaked after only eight years and then went again into decline. Increasingly, higher education is returning to its roots as a private good.

So what are we to take away from this story of the rise and fall of the Cold War university? One conclusion is that the golden age of the American university in the mid-twentieth century was a one-off event. Wars may be endemic, but the Cold War was unique. So American university administrators and professors need to stop pining for a return to the good old days and learn how to live in the post–Cold War era.

The good news is that the impact of the surge in public investment in higher education has left the system in a radically stronger condition than it was in before the Second World War. Enrollments have gone from 1.5 million to 21 million; federal research funding has gone from near zero to $135 billion; federal grants and loans to college students have gone from near zero to $170 billion.[25] And the American system of colleges and universities went from an international also-ran to a powerhouse in the world economy of higher education. Even though all of the numbers are now dropping, they are dropping from a very high level, which is the legacy of the Cold War. So really, we academics should stop whining. We should just say thanks to the bomb for all that it did for us and move on.

The bad news, of course, is that the numbers really are going down. Government funding for research is declining, and there is no prospect for a turnaround in the foreseeable future. This is a problem because the federal government is the primary source of funds for basic research in the United States; corporations are only interested in investing in research that yields immediate dividends. During the Cold War, research universities developed a business model that depended heavily on external research funds to support faculty, graduate students, and overhead. That model is now broken. The cost of pursuing a college education is increasingly being borne by the students themselves, as states are paying a declining share of the costs of higher education. Tuition is rising, and as a result student loans are rising. Public research universities are in a particularly difficult position because their state funding is falling most rapidly. According to one estimate, at the current rate of decline, the average state fiscal support for public higher education will reach zero in 2059.[26]

Consider how this leaves the U.S. system of higher education in comparison to systems in the rest of the developed world. According to data from the Organisation for Economic Co-operation and Development (OECD), the United States spends an enormous amount on higher education—2.6 percent of gross domestic product, compared to 1.6 percent for the OECD average (equaled only by South Korea).[27] Of this total, 38 percent in the United States comes from public sources and 62 percent from private sources, whereas in the OECD generally this ratio is reversed, with 70 percent coming from public sources and 30 percent from private sources. In addition, 45 percent of the costs of higher education in the United States come from households.[28] Individual consumers pay the primary freight.

> In the U.S., the total cost for an individual to obtain a higher education is quite large. On average, the total cost for a man in the U.S. to pursue higher education is more than USD 116 000—about USD 71 000 in direct costs, and USD 45 000 in foregone earnings while he is in school. Only three other countries have total costs that exceed USD 100 000: Japan (USD 103 965), the Netherlands (USD 104 231), and the United Kingdom (USD 122 555). However, in these latter countries, the lion's share of the total costs consists of foregone earnings.[29]

But in the midst of all of this bad news, we need to keep in mind that the American system of higher education has a long history of surviving and even thriving under conditions of at best modest public funding. At its heart, this is a system based on not the state but the market. In the hardscrabble nineteenth century, the system developed mechanisms for getting by without the steady support of funds from church or state. Schools in the system learned how to attract tuition-paying students, give them the college experience they wanted, get them to identify closely with the institution, and then milk them for donations when they graduate. Football, fraternities, logo-bearing T-shirts, and fund-raising operations all paid off handsomely. Colleges and universities learned how to adapt quickly to trends in the competitive environment, whether it's the adoption of intercollegiate athletics, the establishment of research centers to capitalize on funding opportunities, or providing students with lavish exercise facilities and extensive menus of food choices. Public institutions have a long history of behaving much like private institutions because they have never been able to count on continuing state funding.

So, conceived and nurtured into maturity as a private good, the American system of higher education remains a market-based organism. It took the threat of nuclear war to turn it—briefly—into a public good. But those days seem as remote as the time when schoolchildren huddled together in bomb shelters.

8

UPSTAIRS, DOWNSTAIRS

Relations between the Tiers of the System

A common problem with discussions of the American system of higher education is that they tend to focus much too heavily on a few institutions at its very pinnacle. My own book has also fallen into that pattern. In my defense, the lure of the top ranks is compelling. Especially since the system started out in the nineteenth century in such a lowly academic state, its emergence in the twentieth century as a world leader is nothing short of a marvel, which makes it only natural to shine a light on the small number of private and public research universities that dominate the system and occupy the top level of world rankings. Rags to riches stories are hard to resist, and everyone loves a winner. In addition, the institutions at the top have exerted an enormous impact on the institutions below, spurring them to try to move up the ladder or at least to adopt the forms and symbols of the research university.

But now, as I near the end of this analysis, I shift focus toward the lower tiers of the system that account for an overwhelming majority of institutions and enrollments. These are the institutions that define the college experience for most Americans, and they are also the ones that feed the most graduates into the American economy.

To understand these lower-tier colleges we need to keep in mind how rarefied the upper reaches of the system really are. Out of the

4,700 institutions of higher education in the United States, only 191 are selective in admissions, meaning that they accept fewer than half of the students who apply.[1] That's only 4 percent; 96 percent of American colleges accept most applicants. And the selectivity of the top group is actually inflated by the recent pattern (reinforced by the shift toward a standard application form) in which students apply to a large number of competitive colleges in the hope of getting lucky. More than 60 percent of students now apply to four or more colleges. Multiple applications make for lower acceptance rates.[2]

If we look only at the major research universities, the numbers get even smaller. The American Association of Universities (AAU) is the exclusive club for these institutions. With sixty-two members, it accounts for only a little more than 1 percent of all colleges, and, with an undergraduate enrollment of 1.1 million, it includes only 5 percent of all students. But what an influence this small number of institutions has. The AAU accounts for 19 percent of all U.S. graduate students, 46 percent of all research doctorates, 58 percent of all federal research and development grants, 63 percent of all scholars elected to the American Academy of Arts and Sciences, and 71 percent of all U.S. Nobel prize winners. In addition, its graduates occupy the centers of power, including fifty-eight of the current Fortune 100 CEOs, twenty-one current governors, 238 current members of Congress, and, since 1900 (when U.S. universities started to come into their own) twelve U.S. presidents and forty-four Supreme Court justices. Between 2008 and 2012, these universities produced 1.2 million publications and earned 12.8 million academic citations.[3]

What the Lower Tiers Mean for Students

So this tiny group of leading universities does deserve a lot of attention because of the disproportionate role these institutions play in American academic, economic, cultural, social, and political life. Acknowledged. But, still, where does this leave the 99 percent of colleges and universities that are neither highly selective nor strongly research oriented—and the twenty million students who attend them? How do both students and professors negotiate a system as highly stratified as this one?

Let's start with students. Attending an elite college (or even just getting admitted to one) gives a huge boost to a student's chances for high position, but this still leaves a lot of room for others. One study looked at graduates of the top 1 percent of four-year colleges (twenty-eight in total), business schools (twelve), and law schools (twelve), ranked by test scores (SAT, MCAT, LSAT). These included all of the brand-name institutions that are the obsession of upper-middle-class parents bracing themselves for the college admissions wars. The study's author found that 39 percent of Fortune 500 CEOs graduated from one of these institutions at either the undergraduate or graduate levels; 13 percent graduated from Harvard alone.[4] Impressive. But this still means that 61 percent of the heads of America's leading corporations graduated from colleges with less-elevated pedigrees. So apparently institutions without the glamorous brand also offer access to positions at the very top of American society.

But of course, the numbers I've been presenting so far are only focused on higher ed for the tippy-top of American society, the 1 percent of the 1 percent. Most students are not going to college in order to join the executive suite or the Supreme Court. They're just looking for a good white-collar job—a step or two up from the positions held by their parents—which will provide a comfortable salary, good benefits, tolerable working conditions, and a modicum of security. So, for example, let's consider the prospects for getting a job at a tech company in Silicon Valley. A study of the college affiliations of tech company employees on LinkedIn shows that the pipeline to a job at Google or Facebook runs through the two biggest-name universities in the Bay Area, Stanford and Berkeley. Advantage elites. But it also shows that at Apple the largest number of employees graduated from San José State, a nonselective regional state university (and former normal school), which accepts 60 percent of applicants (compared with 5 percent at Stanford and 17 percent at Berkeley).[5] Another analysis paints an even brighter picture for graduates of lower-tier universities. The recruiting platform Jobvite examined seven million applications for 40,000 positions at tech clients such as Twitter and LinkedIn. An article in *Business Insider* published the results with the title "The 20 Universities That Are Most Likely to Land You a Job in Silicon Valley." Number one, it turns out, was San José State. San Francisco State (with a 66 percent admit rate) was number three; Berkeley was second and Stanford fourth.[6] You can understand why the San José State website bears the motto Powering Silicon Valley.

Also, keep in mind that both of the California State University campuses admit as many community college transfers every year as they do freshmen.[7] So this means that a sizable number of community college graduates are also getting access to jobs at major tech companies. As you may recall, these two lower tiers of the American system of higher education educate 77 percent of all undergraduates, 39 percent at open-access universities and 38 percent at two-year colleges. Therefore the story is not just that there is hope of getting a good job for students who don't attend one of the schools in the top 1 percent; it's that there is also hope for students in the system's bottom three quartiles.

The point here is not that the American system of higher education is egalitarian. In fact, as we have seen, it is extraordinarily stratified. Instead, the point is that the system's hierarchical structure arose from the bottom up, out of the competition among colleges for students, resources, and esteem. It was not dictated from above by government fiat. By the time the state of California put its master plan for higher education into place in the 1960s, it was only institutionalizing a three-tier structure that had already established itself over time—with research universities at the top (UC), community colleges at the bottom (CCC), and teaching-oriented universities in the middle (CSU). And at the same time the plan reinforced the system's existing informal pattern of upward mobility, by mandating that both university systems allocate a large number of slots for community college transfers. The result is a system that is both radically unequal—with the different levels offering sharply different programs, opportunities, prestige, and exclusivity—and relatively fluid.

Instead of allocating access to the top level of the system using the mechanism employed by most of the rest of the world—a state-administered university matriculation exam—the highly decentralized American system allocates access by means of informal mechanisms that in comparison seem anarchic. In the absence of a single access route, there are many; and in the absence of clear rules for prospective students, there are multiple and conflicting rules of thumb. Also, the rules of thumb vary radically according to which tier of the system you are seeking to enter.

First, let's look at the admissions process for families (primarily the upper-middle class) who are trying to get their children entrée to the elite category of highly selective liberal arts colleges and research universities. They have to take into account the wide array of factors that enter into the complex and opaque process that American colleges use to select students at this level: quality of high school; quality of a student's program of study; high school grades; test scores in the SAT or ACT; interests and passions expressed in an application essay; parents' alumni status; whether the student needs financial aid; athletic skills; service activities; diversity factors such as race, ethnicity, class, national origin, gender, and sexual orientation; and extracurricular contributions a student might make to the college community. There is no centralized review process; instead, every college carries out its own admissions review and employs its own criteria.

This open and indeterminate process provides a huge advantage for upper-middle-class families. If you are a parent who is a college graduate and who works at a professional or managerial job, where the payoff of going to a good college is readily apparent, you have the cultural and social capital to negotiate this system effectively and read its coded messages. For you, going to college is not the issue; it's a matter of which college your children can get into that would provide them with the greatest competitive advantage in the workplace. You want for them the college that might turn them down rather than the one that would welcome them with open arms. So you enroll your children in test prep, hire a college adviser, plan out a strategic plan for high school course taking and extracurriculars, craft a service résumé that makes them look appropriately public spirited, take them on the obligatory college tour, and come up with just the right mix of applications to the stretch schools, the safety schools, and those in between. And all this pays off handsomely: 77 percent of children from families in the top quintile by income gain a bachelor's degree.[8]

If you are a parent farther down the class scale, who didn't attend college and whose own work environment is not well stocked with college graduates, you have a lot more trouble negotiating the system. The odds are not good: for students from the fourth income quintile, only 17 percent earn a BA, and for the lowest quintile the rate is only 9 percent.[9] Under these circumstances, having your child go to a college, any college, is a big deal, and one college is hard to distinguish from another. But you are faced with a system that offers an extraordinary diversity of choices for prospective students: public, not-for-profit, or for-profit; two-year or four-year; college or university; teaching or research oriented; massive or tiny student body; vocational or liberal; division I, II, or III intercollegiate athletics, or no sports at all; party school or nerd haven; high rank or low rank; full-time or part-time enrollment; urban or pastoral; gritty or serene; residential, commuter, or "suitcase college" (where students go home on weekends). In this complex setting, both consumers and providers somehow have to make choices that are in their own best interest. Families from the upper-middle class are experts at negotiating this system, trimming the complexity down to a few essentials: a four-year institution that is highly selective and preferably private (not-for-profit). Everything else is optional.

If you're part of a working-class family, however—lacking deep knowledge of the system and without access to the wide array of support systems that money can buy—you are more likely to take the system at face value. Having your children go to a community college is the most obvious and attractive option. It's close to home, inexpensive, and easy to get into. It's where your children's friends will be going, it allows them to work and go to school part time, and it doesn't seem as forbiddingly alien as the state university (much less the Ivies). You don't need anything to gain admission except a high school diploma or GED. No tests, counselors, tours, or résumé burnishing is required. Or you could try the next step up, the local comprehensive state university. To apply for admission, all you need is a high school transcript. You might get turned down, but the odds are in your favor. The cost is higher than for a community college but can usually be paid with federal grants and loans. An alternative is a for-profit institution, which is extremely accessible, flexible, and often online. It's not cheap, but federal grants and loans can pay the cost. What you may not know, however, is that the most accessible colleges at the bottom of the system are also the ones where students are least likely to graduate. (Only 29 percent of students entering two-year colleges earn an associate degree in three years; only 39 percent earn a degree from a two-year or four-year institution in six years.)[10] You also may not be aware that the economic payoff for these colleges is lower or that the colleges higher up the system may provide stronger support toward graduation and might even be less expensive because of greater scholarship funding.

In this way, the complexity and opacity of this market-based and informally structured system helps reinforce the social advantages of those at the top of the social ladder and limit the opportunities for those at the bottom. It's a system that rewards the insider knowledge of old hands and punishes newcomers. To work it effectively, you need to reject the fiction that a college is a college is a college and learn how seek advantage in the system's upper tiers.

At the same time, however, the system's fluidity is real. The absence of state-sanctioned and formally structured tracks means that the barriers between the system's tiers are permeable. Your children's futures are not predetermined by their high school curriculums or their scores on matriculation exams. They can apply to any college they want and see what happens. Of course, if their grades and scores are not great, their chances of admission to upper-level institutions are poor. But their chances of getting into a teaching-oriented state university are pretty good, and their chances of getting into a community college are virtually assured. And if they take the latter option, as is most often the case for children from socially disadvantaged families, there is a real (if modest) possibility that they might be able to prove their academic chops, earn an AA degree, and transfer to a university, even a research university. The probabilities of moving up in the system are low: most community college students never earn an AA degree, and transfers have a harder time succeeding in the university than students who enroll there as freshmen. But the possibilities are nonetheless genuine.

Notice that I'm taking the argument from chapter 5—that the system provides both social access and social advantage—and showing how this combination of functions is a major source of strength for the system. American higher education offers something for everyone. It helps those at the bottom to get ahead and those at the top to stay ahead. It provides socially useful educational services for every ability level and every consumer preference. This gives it an astonishingly broad base of political support across the entire population, since everyone needs it and everyone can potentially benefit from it. And this kind of legitimacy is not attainable if the opportunity the system offers to the lower classes is a simple fraud. First-generation college students, even if they struggled in high school, can attend community college, transfer to San José State, and end up working at the coolest and most valuable corporation in the world. It's not very likely, but it assuredly is possible. True, the more advantages you bring to the system—cultural capital, connections, family wealth—the higher the probability that you will succeed in it. But even if you are lacking in these attributes, there is still an outside chance that you just might make it through the system and emerge with a good middle-class job.

This helps explain how the system gets away with preserving social advantage for those at the top without stirring a revolt from those at the bottom. Students from working-class and lower-class families are much less likely to be admitted to the upper reaches of the higher education system that provides the greatest social rewards, but the opportunity to attend some form of college is high, and attending a college at the lower levels of the system may provide access to a good job. The combination of high access to the lower levels of the system and high attrition on the way to attaining a bachelor's degree creates a situation where the system gets credit for openness and the student bears the burden for failing to capitalize on it. The system gave you a chance, but you just couldn't make the grade. The ready-made explanations for personal failure accumulate quickly as students try to move through the system. You didn't study hard enough, you didn't get good grades in high school, and you didn't get good test scores, so you couldn't get into a selective college. Instead you went to a community college, where you got distracted from your studies by work, family, and friends, and you didn't have the necessary academic ability, so you failed to complete your AA degree. Or maybe you did complete the degree and transferred to a university, but you had trouble competing with students who were more able and better prepared than you. Along with the majority of students who don't make it all the way to a BA, you bear the burden for your failure—a conclusion that is reinforced by the occasional but highly visible successes of a few of your peers. The system is well defended against charges of unfairness.

So we can understand why people at the bottom don't cry foul. It gave you a chance. And there is one more reason for keeping up your hope that education will pay off for you. A degree from an institution in a lower tier may pay lower benefits, but for some purposes one degree really is as good as another. Often the question in getting a job or a promotion is not whether you have a classy credential but whether you have whatever credential is listed as the minimum requirement in the job description. Bureaucracies operate on a level where form often matters more than substance. As long as you can check off the box confirming that you have a bachelor's degree, the BA from University of Phoenix and the BA from University of Pennsylvania can serve the same function, by allowing you to be considered for the job. And if, say, you're a public school teacher, an MA from Capella University, under the district contract, is as effective as one from Berkeley, because either will qualify you for a $5,000 bump in pay.

At the same time, however, we can see why the system generates so much anxiety among students who are trying to use the system to move up the social ladder for the good life. It's really the only game in town for getting a good job in twenty-first-century America. Without higher education, you are closed off from the white-collar jobs that provide the most security and pay. Yes, you could try to start a business, or, without a college degree, you could try to work your way up the ladder in an organization. But the first approach is highly risky and the second is highly unlikely, since most jobs come with minimum education requirements regardless of experience. So you have to put all of your hopes in the higher-ed basket while knowing—because of your own difficult experiences in high school and because of what you see happening with family and friends—that your chances for success are not good. Either you choose to pursue higher ed against the odds or you simply give up. It's a situation fraught with anxiety.

What is less obvious, however, is why the American system of higher education—which is so clearly skewed in favor of people at the top of the social order—fosters so much anxiety for these people. Upper-middle-class families in the United States are obsessed with education and especially with getting their children into the right college. Why? They live in the communities that have the best public schools; their children have cultural and social skills that schools value and reward; and they can afford the direct cost and opportunity cost of sending their high school grads to a residential college, even one of the pricey privates. So why are there only a few colleges that seem to matter to this group? Why does it matter so much to have your child not only get into the University of California but into Berkeley or UCLA? What's wrong with having them attend Riverside or even one of the Cal State campuses? And why the overwhelming passion for pursuing admission to Harvard or Yale?

The urgency behind all such frantic concern about admission to the most elite level of the system is this: as parents of privilege, you can pass on your wealth to your children, but you can't give them a profession. Education is built into the core of modern societies, where occupations are no longer inherited but more or less earned. If you're a successful doctor or lawyer, you can provide a lot of advantages for your children, but in order for them to gain a position such as yours, they must succeed in high school, get into a good college, and then into a good graduate school. Unless they own the company, even business executives can't pass on position to their children, and even then it's increasingly rare that they would actually do so. (Like most shareholders, they would profit more by having the company led by a competent executive than by the boss's son.) Under these circumstances of modern life, providing social advantage to your children means providing them with educational advantage. Parents who have been through the process of climbing the educational hierarchy in order to gain prominent position in the occupational hierarchy know full well what it takes to make the grade.

They also know something else: when you're at the top of the social system, there is little opportunity to rise higher but plenty of opportunity to fall farther down. Consider data on intergenerational mobility in the United States. For children of parents in the top quintile by household income, 60 percent end up at least one quintile lower than their parents and 37 percent fall at least two quintiles.[11] That's a substantial decline in social position. So there's good reason for these parents to fear downward mobility for their children and to use all their powers to marshal educational resources to head it off. The problem is that, even though your own children have a wealth of advantages in negotiating the educational system, there are still enough bright and ambitious students from the lower classes who manage to make it through the educational gauntlet to pose them a serious threat. So you need to make sure that your children attend the best elementary schools, get into the high-level reading group and the program for the gifted, take plenty of advanced placement classes, and then get into a highly selective college and graduate school. Leave nothing to chance, since some of your heirs are likely to be less talented and ambitious than those children who prove themselves against all odds by climbing the educational ladder. When the higher education system opened up access after World War II, it made competition for the top tier of the system sharply higher, and the degree of competitiveness continued to increase as the proportion of students going to college grew to a sizable majority. As Jerome Karabel has noted in his study of elite college admissions, the American system of higher education does not equalize opportunity but it does equalize anxiety.[12] It makes families at all levels of American society nervous about their ability to negotiate the system effectively, because it provides the only highway to the good life.

What the Lower Tiers Mean for Faculty

The multiple tiers of the American higher education system have important implications not only for students but also for faculty. One imperative for the system is to reproduce itself. It needs to graduate a sufficient number of people with doctoral degrees who have the ability and motivation to fill the more than 1.5 million faculty positions at the country's 4,700 colleges and universities.[13] So, for a moment, let's shift analytical direction and look at the system from the perspective of professors. First, consider the problem that the professoriate poses for the success and legitimacy of the higher education system as a whole. In a radically stratified system such as America's, where the greatest rewards and privileges are heavily weighted toward the research universities and liberal arts colleges in the top tier, institutions in the lower tiers somehow need to be able to recruit and retain capable faculty members, many of whom are really dying to be at Harvard. If these institutions don't manage this trick, they will become intellectual backwaters that will not be able to deliver, even in part, on the system's promise to give students in the lower tiers educational opportunities that will allow access to a middle-class job. As it turns out, the solution to this dilemma can be found in the fact that, in the American system of higher education, students and faculty find themselves in a strikingly similar situation.

As we have seen, the system offers students the possibility of upward mobility through higher education, but the probability for students to attain a substantial rise in social position is low. A substantial number will wash out of the system with no degree and major debt. Others will attain a degree at a lower tier and move into a lower-tier white-collar job; some will gain a degree that ushers them into a middle-tier position; and a few will grab the brass ring. It's much the same with faculty.

The math facing prospective faculty members who seek a position at the top of the system is daunting. There are 108 universities in the United States classified as "very high research" institutions, which produce most of the research doctoral degrees, and nearly half of these

degrees are granted by the sixty-two universities in the more prestigious AAU. Meanwhile, there are about 2,900 four-year colleges that
seek to hire professors with PhDs. (For community college faculty,
the minimum requirement for employment is normally an MA.) Of
more than one million faculty positions at four-year institutions, only
7 percent are at AAU universities and 20 percent are at very high
research universities.[14] So at the moment of graduation, PhD holders
from AAU institutions who seek a faculty position face an academic
job market where 93 percent of the potential faculty positions will be
at a lower tier of the system than the one that educated them—often
a much lower tier. For graduates of very high research universities,
80 percent of the likely jobs are at a lower level. Downward mobility
is the fate for the large majority of candidates for the professoriate.

Actually, if you look at the figures at the very top of the system,
the math is even more daunting. As you may recall from chapter 6,
Val Burris examined all ninety-four departments in the United States
that offered PhDs in sociology and traced their patterns of hiring each
other's graduates. He found that the five top-ranked departments supplied 32 percent of the faculty for all ninety-four and hired 56 percent
of their own faculty from other top-five departments; only 9 percent
of top-five faculty came from schools below the top twenty. Meanwhile, the top twenty departments provided 69 percent of all faculty
in the ninety-four. Of top-five grads who got jobs in the top ninety-
four, 14 percent went to departments in the top five and 65 percent to
the departments ranked below twenty. For graduates of departments
ranked lower than twenty who got jobs in these ninety-four departments, 90 percent ended up in departments ranked below twenty.[15]

Consider what this means for prospective professors. If you want
a faculty position in one of the top five departments, you'd be well
advised to get your degree from one of these institutions. If you want
a decent shot at a top-twenty job, you'll need a top-twenty degree. But
even graduates of the most elite schools experience major downward
mobility. For candidates with top-five degrees who found jobs in the
top ninety-four departments, two-thirds ended up in departments
that were below the twentieth rank. And this doesn't include those

who might have found positions in one of the 2,800 four-year colleges ranked below the top ninety-four.

Of course, a lot of people never succeed in finding a faculty position at all. A 1999 study surveyed thousands of PhD recipients about their faculty search experience ten years after degree. Just over half said they wanted to be professors, but after ten years, less than two-thirds of those people had attained a faculty position and only half had gained a tenured position.[16] Given the numbers we have already seen about where faculty positions are available, the large majority of the prospective faculty members who achieve their goal do so at an institution that is below the rank of the university where they gained their PhD, and most will be in colleges and universities that are neither selective nor research oriented. In fact, a sizable number of graduates end one tier farther down the hierarchy, not in a four-year institution at all but in a two-year community college. More than a quarter of all college faculty members teach at community colleges, and 16 percent of the full-time faculty in these institutions have PhDs.[17] Oh yes, and then there is one more big problem facing PhD holders seeking faculty positions: of the one million or so faculty members at four-year colleges and universities, many are working part time—including 35 percent at public institutions and 50 percent at private institutions, percentages that have been steadily climbing over that last quarter century.[18] Part-time status means low pay, no security, and no benefits. In 2011, the median pay for an adjunct to teach a class at a public research university was $3,200.[19]

Think about where this leaves prospective professors who receive their PhD from an institution that is not ranked in the top twenty. The vast oversupply of elite degree holders compared to elite faculty positions leads to a cascade of downward mobility, as elite degrees bump aside less elite degrees in the competition for positions all the way down the extended hierarchy of America's system of higher education. As a result, graduates of the top research institutions monopolize hiring at those institutions and heavily populate faculties at less research-oriented universities, and graduates of lesser research universities come to fill the faculties at the teaching-oriented four-year colleges and universities that serve the largest number of students. Those who are left take a part-time position at one or more four-year institutions or find a job at a community college. At this point, finally, consider the virtually hopeless situation facing prospective professors who earned their degree from one of the 460 institutions granting research PhDs that are not in the very high research category, institutions that produce 34 percent of all American research doctorates.[20]

For recent doctoral graduates, the fall from grace can be breathtaking, as they leave the hallowed confines of elite institutions—with their low teaching loads, heavy focus on graduate students, selective admissions, and ample support for research—to the real world of regional state universities, where classes are large, course loads are heavy, the students are undergrads, selectivity is low, and time and resources for research are scarce. As a result, in all likelihood new doctoral graduates end up in jobs they don't want.

So how do they handle this situation? Consider things from their point of view. First off, you immediately launch a campaign to claw your way up through the ranks of institutions toward the tier of research universities from which you recently emerged. And the strategy for accomplishing this is well established: you have to write your way into a better job. Prove yourself as a scholar who is worthy of a faculty position in a research institution. The early years, however, can be tenuous and fluid. Maybe you find no faculty position at all in the beginning, so you look for a postdoctoral position that will allow you to publish. Or you put off graduation, in order to work on publications and keep your degree from going stale. Or you take on a temporary contract position or several part-time posts in the hope that one may turn into a permanent job.

Then, once you find a permanent position in the wrong institution, you try to parlay it into a permanent job at the right one. First, you build on the research in your doctoral dissertation, seeking to present it at conferences and move pieces of it toward publication in the best academic journals or university presses you can get to accept them. Then you quickly develop a new line of research, which relates to your dissertation work but moves it in a promising new direction, and you work assiduously to get this work published in the right places so it will earn you the attention of senior scholars in your field. Network like crazy, drawing on your adviser's stature and contacts and developing your own web of scholars, to whom you introduce your work in the hope of enlisting them as champions. Apply for grants to support your work, buy out some of your teaching time, and pay for research assistants, knowing also that grant getting is one of the critical academic skills that search committees at research universities are looking for in junior faculty candidates. Get yourself nominated for dissertation awards and early career awards, which can serve as signals to the market that you're primed for stardom. All of this is going to be difficult, not just because of the fierce competition with recent PhDs like yourself, but because you're in an institution with a heavy teaching load and little support for research. All the same, with luck, connections, and a strong publication record, you may win a position farther up the status ladder. Congratulations. Now you need to get tenure in this new more competitive environment. If you fail, you get bumped down the ladder again. And there is no starting over.

This is a difficult process, and the chances of succeeding are not good. In particular, few people manage to get all the way back to the level of the university from which they graduated. But moving up a step or two is a real possibility, and the benefits are measurable. Such a move brings a higher salary, lighter teaching load, greater institutional support for your research, better students, more graduate students who can serve as research assistants, and a better letterhead to use in applying for the next position. At the beginning, it helps a lot to have a degree from a stellar institution, but over time you increasingly rely on the number and quality of your publications to demonstrate your ability. And over time your status is less defined by the label of the university that provided your degree and more by the label of the college where you are currently teaching.

At a certain point, a few years out from graduation, your position in the hierarchy becomes fixed. Your letterhead has become your scholarly identity. Now what? The next logical step is to try to make your current institution more like the one you graduated from and continue to long for. So you and your similarly situated colleagues pressure the administration to move the institution itself up the status ladder of higher education. The strategy for accomplishing institutional mobility is similar to the strategy for pursuing personal mobility. You push to lower teaching loads, hire more research-oriented faculty, increase the research standards for tenure and promotion, increase salaries for the most productive scholars, increase research and travel funds, make undergraduate admissions more selective, increase the size of graduate programs, and, if possible, set up a doctoral program. Administration, faculty colleagues, students, and alumni are likely to be of the same mind in urging the university to move up the rankings, since everyone benefits from association with a more prestigious institution. With all parties comfortably grandfathered in, they all can revel in being part of an organization whose rising standards would no longer allow it to admit anyone like themselves. For most actors in the institution, there really is no downside to affiliation with an upwardly mobile college.

What does this mean for students in the lower tiers? First, let's look at the impact of faculty mobility, moving down and back up in the system, then at the impact of faculty efforts to raise the college in the rankings. On the positive side, the faculty mobility system sets things up so that colleges and universities in the lower tiers are heavily populated with highly qualified faculty. The best doctoral programs produce a lot of faculty for the lesser institutions in the hierarchy. As a result, downward mobility for faculty can promote upward mobility for students, as students get the advantage of a potentially first-rate education via professors who have experienced this kind of education themselves. The system dispatches its newly minted scholars from the research university to the academic hinterlands in the lower tiers, as talent from the system's top trickles down toward the bottom. Students in the lower tiers get access to some of the educational benefits from elite universities that would never admit them to its own programs.

The problem with this system for students is that they often get faculty who would rather be somewhere else—who want to work with better students at a higher degree level and who are trying to contain their teaching duties so they can write themselves into a better job. In addition, these faculty come from a privileged educational background that makes it difficult for them to work with students whose educational profile is more middle-of-the-pack. Also, the faculty rose to the top of what they see as a rigorous educational meritocracy, which makes it hard for them not to look down on the students at open-access colleges as inherently less worthy. This is not a healthy basis for a teacher-student relationship.

Faculty not only try to move up the system personally, but they also try to raise the level of the institution they are in. The positive side of this for students is that they, too, get to ride the college up the ladder. Even after they graduate, a rise in ranking elevates their own credentials in the marketplace. Also, as we saw in chapter 3, over time, students in the lower-tier institutions, which usually started out as relatively narrowly vocational in orientation, became exposed to an increasingly liberal education, which provided a broader range of learning and offered a wider range of occupational opportunities. But the problem for students with this shift in college orientation is that, instead of getting a strong educational background in a particular occupational domain, they may find themselves consuming a watered-down version of an elite liberal curriculum, which potentially provides them with neither a rich cultural education nor a useful entry point into the workforce. It may not be in the best interests of students in regional state universities to enroll in programs that are essentially Harvard Lite.

So, where does this leave us? Like so much else about the American system of higher education, the relationship between the lower and upper tiers of the system bring both students and faculty a combination of outcomes that are a mix of good news and bad news. The system offers both of them the possibility of getting ahead and, simultaneously, the probability of not getting ahead very far if at all. The opportunities are real, and so is the likelihood that in the end most people who start with advantages will end up advantaged and most people who start out disadvantaged will end up the same way. It motivates both to pursue opportunity, and, if they don't succeed, it saddles both with the blame for failure. We gave you the chance, it says, but you just couldn't hack it. As always, the system lets us have things both ways: access and advantage, opportunity and privilege, mobility and stasis.

9

A PERFECT MESS

Over the last two centuries, the American system of higher education has had an extraordinary ride. It started in as an ignominious collection of colleges with state charters but few prospects. Located on the fringe of a frontier society and lacking a reliable source of financial support, they had to struggle just to survive. They managed to do so by hiring faculty who would work for marginal pay, seeking out students who (whatever their academic abilities) could pay full tuition, attracting donations from alumni and local businessmen who saw value in a college connection, and begging for handouts from church and state. The founders of these colleges were not seeking to promote higher learning. At best, they were trying to prepare clergy and promote a particular religious denomination in the competitive zone of expanding development. At worst, they were just trying to pump up the value of their landholdings in a setting where there was too much land and too few settlers, where establishing a college was a way to lure property buyers by making a nothing town look like a center of culture.

By the 1880s, with five times as many colleges as all of Europe, the system had vast numbers but little drawing power and no academic respect. Only with the rapid adoption of the research university model in the late nineteenth century did this ragtag collection of lackluster institutions start to gain a modicum of credibility. Yet, although this model promised academic excellence and cutting-edge knowledge production, for the next fifty years there was little of either to be found at most American institutions of higher education. Instead, the driving force for the huge expansion of college enrollments in the early twentieth century was less the lust for learning than the lure of earning. College had become the primary mechanism for middle-class families to pass on social advantage to their children and for working-class families to give their children access to middle-class jobs.

The result was a century-long surge in consumer demand for higher education that fostered a massive increase in the system's size and complexity. The largest increase in demand came during the Cold War, when most of the new enrollments occurred at the newer open-access institutions in the lower tiers of the system's hierarchy. It was also during this period that the exclusive research-intensive institutions in the system's top tier claimed their current position as the most prestigious universities in the world. Altogether, the 100-year rise of the American system of higher education—from poverty and disdain in the nineteenth century to riches and acclaim in the twentieth—is one of the all-time great institutional success stories. As a result, competitors around the world have been working hard to move up the global rankings by adopting elements of the American model: things like transferable credits, standardized degree programs, student tuition charges, institutional autonomy, competitive research grants, incentives for faculty to do research, institutional ranking systems, and metrics for academic citations and journal quality.

In light of this amazing rise, the American system of higher education in the early twenty-first century should be basking in the glow of accomplishments. On the contrary, however, in a number of ways the system's situation today is dicey. Its great success has been causing it problems. It has expanded enormously to meet the demands of educational consumers, who want to use it to get ahead and stay ahead. But now the costs for consumers and for the state have come to seem too high, so the rate of growth in enrollments has been slowing, as state appropriations fall and tuition rises along with student loan debts. This trend, in turn, is seen as posing a potential threat to the great hope for equal opportunity that American education has long offered. Americans are attuned to think that social inequality is OK as long as social opportunity is wide open, and education is how we have long provided such opportunity.

College is the segment of the larger educational system that is currently the primary locus of opportunity; now that the lower levels of the educational system are full, it is the only place where people can gain opportunity and preserve advantage. But undergraduate enrollments are gradually nearing the point of universality, and this means that the zone of advantage is moving up another level to graduate school. The number of graduate degrees conferred every year has risen to half the number of bachelor's degrees, following the long pattern of American educational expansion.[1] To keep going like this seems prohibitively expensive, but to stop seems politically and socially unthinkable, signaling the death of the American Dream.

As a result, American higher education, which has long been the crown jewel of the larger educational system, is now becoming tarnished by increasingly sharp criticism and threatened by radical reform proposals. Historically this is the fate of whatever level of the system is in the process of filling up with students. It was what happened to the elementary school in the nineteenth century and the high school in the twentieth century. In the twenty-first century we now hear calls for greater accountability about the benefits colleges produce, for greater transparency in how colleges work and how they use their money, and for unbundling all of the complex activities and functions of the university and providing them through organizations that are leaner and more specialized. There are calls to reduce costs by outsourcing instruction through online courses, increasing teaching loads, and getting rid of the fluff, such as lush campuses and football.

Overall, these calls for change appear very sensible. The reason for this is that, on the face of it, the system as a whole—and the full-service university in particular—are hard to defend in a credible manner. Many of the system's central operating principles—such as extreme organizational complexity, operational opacity, and a strange mix of highbrow knowledge and lowbrow athletics—simply lack face validity. Yet I argue that these very characteristics, legacies of the system's origins, are the central elements in making the American higher education system so successful.

As we have seen, the system emerged in a time when the state was weak, the market strong, and the church splintered. Its early aims had little to do with first-rate research, high-level learning, social mobility, or economic utility. The early colleges, which established the core rules and structures of the system, were set up to accomplish other less-elevated goals, such as to promote sectarian influence, enhance property values, and provide bragging rights for one town over another. The result was a flexible, durable, entrepreneurial, and consumer-oriented system of higher education. But the substantive problem is that this system of higher education did not arise in order to provide education, and for a long time what education it did provide was not very high.

I suggest, however, that these unlikely origins are what have made the American system of higher education so successful. It succeeded by doing everything wrong. It's a system without a plan, which emerged in response to a set of market-based incentives that were peculiar to a particular time and place—the early nineteenth-century United States. Since no governing entity had the will, the power, or the money to control its development, the system fumbled along on its own. It learned how to adapt to contingency, take advantage of opportunity, survive in the face of adversity, seek out sources of financial and political support, accumulate a variety of social functions and forms of legitimacy, please major constituencies, and develop a loyal and generous group of alumni.

As with a lot of market-based institutions, it was rigid in its focus on the need to survive, while being quite flexible over the years about how to justify its existence in the face of changing contexts and constituencies. At various times, and all at the same time, it has existed in order to promote the faith, enrich developers, boost civic pride, educate leaders, produce human capital, develop knowledge, provide opportunity, promote advantage, supply a pleasant interlude between childhood and adulthood, help people meet the right spouse, expand the economy, and enhance state power. Oh, and, yes, it has also served as a minor league for professional sports, a major venue for public entertainment, and a massive jobs program.

Defining Elements of the American System of Higher Education

What are the elements of the American system of higher education that were key in enabling it to become so successful in such a short period of time? One of these elements is *institutional autonomy*. Around the world, most universities are wholly owned subsidiaries of the state. The state owns, funds, and governs these universities, treating them much like other local offices of a government agency and treating their faculty members much like other civil servants. Budgets, pay levels, fees, admissions, policies, and programs all derive from mandates by the national or provincial ministries of education. But in the United States, colleges and universities tend to operate like independent entrepreneurial enterprises in a competitive market environment. Policy and funding at public institutions are under greater state constraints than at private institutions, but the gap between the two is more a matter of degree than a categorical chasm. State funds pay only a portion of the costs at public universities, so the latter have to hustle for alternative sources of funding much like their private counterparts. The relative autonomy of institutions makes the system remarkably flexible, as administrators and faculty are attuned to chasing emerging opportunities, seeking out new markets, and providing new programs and services.

A related core trait of the system is its *sensitivity to consumers*. Unable to depend on the state or the church for full support, universities turn for help to its customer base. Students, especially undergraduates, provide tuition dollars that are a fundamental part of the university budget. In addition to gaining funds directly from students and their families, public colleges and universities also often earn state funds as a function of student enrollments; more students mean more state appropriations. And just as important, graduates of these institutions became a major source of donations, building up endowments and putting their names on new buildings, programs, and professorships. This means that to survive and thrive American colleges need to be able to compete successfully with their peers to attract students, and they also need to make the college experience so compelling and personally formative that graduates will maintain a deep, lifelong loyalty to the institution. So a vibrant and active alumni association—complete with an alumni magazine, annual reunions, homecoming football events, college clubs, and alumni travel offerings—is an important adjunct to the college's development office and a major source of institutional capital. Here is where extracurricular activities—and especially football and basketball—play such an important role, by bonding students to the institution for life and energizing them to wear the colors on game day. As they say at my former institution Michigan State ("go green, go white"), the staunchest alumni "bleed green."

The consumer orientation of the American university provides a window into a broader trait that helps explain its success: its ability to appeal to a *broad array of constituencies*. Because of the intensity of competition in the higher education market—where supply has always exceeded demand—an American university can never afford to put all its chips on one vision of what the institution should be. Instead it needs to serve a multiplicity of functions, however contradictory they may be, and to meet the needs of a variety of constituent groups, however at odds they may be.

As we have seen, the university presents itself simultaneously as a place that is *populist, practical, and elite*. In populist mode, it provides access for a large number of students to an undergraduate experience that is more fulfilling socially than it is demanding academically. This is the university of football games, frat parties, and food courts, which brings in the current tuition dollars and future donations that support the higher learning pursued by faculty and grad students. It is also the part of the university that provides it with the broadest political base in the region and the state, that makes it less the remote ivory tower and more the accessible institution that the public can identify with and root for.

In practical mode, the university provides inventions, programs, and services that are useful to a broad array of people, businesses, and interests. It trains teachers, doctors, and engineers; it produces drugs, software, and strains of wheat; it provides concerts, museums, and plays. It stimulates the economy by hiring a large number of skilled and unskilled employees and by stimulating corporate spinoffs and industrial parks—think Silicon Valley.

In elite mode, the university is the primary locus for knowledge production. It's where the best minds tackle the toughest intellectual problems and train graduate students to be the next generation of intellectual workers. This is the university at its most academic and its most remote. If this was all it did, the university would lack its current robust political and financial base. If it didn't do this at all, the university would be little more than a social club and research and development center. These three elements can be found both within any individual institution—research university, comprehensive university, or community college—and also dispersed differentially across the system as a whole, with the top tier more elite and the lower tiers more populist and practical.

A fourth defining characteristic of the American system of higher education is its *ambiguity*. As a structure, it combines formal equality with informal inequality, a combination that is critically important for its power and legitimacy. A major component of this ambiguity is the murkiness of what it means to "go to college." In the rest of the English-speaking world, going to "college" means attending a lower-tier institution of higher education, more what Americans would call a community college or technical school. The term "university" is reserved for the upper-tier institutions that prepare people for management and the professions. But in the United States the terms "college" and "university" are largely interchangeable. I've been using them this way throughout this book, which has probably been confusing for non-American readers. In common speech, Americans most frequently use the term "college"; saying "university" repeatedly is too multisyllabic and a bit pretentious. American students who are enrolled at Yale say they're going to college. So do students who attend the community college. In this sense, almost all Americans can go to college, and a sizable majority actually do so. But the social benefits of college attendance differ dramatically according to where the college fits into the stratified structure of the system. In the United States, 38 percent of undergraduate students in higher education attend community colleges. Another 39 percent attend nonselective regional state universities. Only 14 percent attend research universities, and only 3 percent attend the private research universities that dominate the rankings.[2] So at the nominal level, the system seems quite accessible and egalitarian, but at the substantive level, it is highly stratified and its benefits radically skewed. Oddly enough, this is a major source of strength for the system, since it fosters a view of higher education as both accessible and exclusive, with community college students donning the cloak of the research university and university students assuming the air of just folks. The result is a system with the broadest possible level of support.

One final trait of the American system of higher education is the *organizational complexity* of individual universities. Actually, to call it complexity is something of an understatement. One influential organizational analysis of universities calls them "organized anarchies," which "can be viewed for some purposes as collections of choices looking for problems, issues and feelings looking for decision situations in which they might be aired, solutions looking for issues to which they might be an answer, and decision makers looking for work."[3] For these scholars, and for me, the organization of universities is functional for its peculiar purposes. But other observers, particularly those in business rather than the academy, have a less flattering view. One long-time businessman who was also a university trustee wrote an opinion piece a few years ago in the *Chronicle of Higher Education* titled "Restoring Sanity to an Academic World Gone Mad," in which he declared, "Never have I observed anything as unfocused or mismanaged as higher education." The reason? "Nobody is in charge."[4]

One source of university complexity, as I explained in chapter 1, is that within this single institution you find a mixture of all three of the radically different forms of authority that have organized social life over the centuries. There is traditional authority, a conservative model grounded in the medieval guild of professors, which in this mode continues to exercise collegial governance over curriculum and instruction. There is charismatic authority, an unstable model subject to the vagaries of individual scholarly genius, which guides the granting of academic ranks, awards, and prestige. And there is rational authority, a modern construction grounded in the rule-based workings of bureaucracy, which efficiently manages the staff, admits and oversees students, and monitors budgets. In theory, the first two forms in modern societies have given way to the third, but in fact universities have granted them all free rein.

Yet another source of complexity in the university comes from the dynamic mix of three quite different organizational structures. One is the structure of departments and schools, where faculty exercise control over hiring, promotion, curriculum, and instruction, protected from both laypeople and from university administrators by the guarantee of tenure. This is the primary source of stability and even stasis within the university, which gives faculty members the security to pursue their intellectual work unhindered by politics or market discipline.

A second is the more fluid and even chaotic structure of academic institutes and centers, which operate outside of the purview of departments and are much more subject to manipulation by central administrators and the fluctuating contingencies of funding opportunities. Departments are forever, but institutes and centers come and go according to the wishes of donors, the enterprise of scholars, priorities of government research funding, and the ambitions of presidents.

A third is central administration, headed by the president and provost. With the president appointed by a lay board of trustees (filled with business people not academics) and with the president appointing everyone else, university administration exerts a much greater power over the university in the United States than elsewhere in the world, exercising final authority over the crucial arenas of faculty appointments and budgets. The president is the prime mediator between university and real world and the mobilizer of external resources for university needs, which makes him a potent counterweight to departments and schools and a major promoter of centers and institutes. As Stanford's president John Hennessey liked to say: college administration may be like herding cats but "I control the cat food." This combination makes for an institution that is both protected from the world and induced to engage with the world, which helps explain both the durability and the adaptability of the American system.

The System's Paradoxical Sources of Strength

What all this means is that the true hero of the story I'm telling about the American system of higher education is not its content but its evolved *form*. All the things we love about it—an intellectual haven in a heartlessly utilitarian world, a font of economic growth, a source of social opportunity, a monument to merit—are all the side effects of a structure that arose for other purposes. The system succeeded by developing a structure that allowed it to become both economically rich and politically autonomous. It could tap multiple sources of revenue and legitimacy, which allowed it to avoid becoming the wholly owned subsidiary of the state, the church, or the market. And by virtue of its structurally reinforced autonomy, college is good for a great many things.

What are those things? For those of us on faculties of American colleges and universities, they provide several core benefits that we see as especially important. At the top of the list is that they preserve and promote free speech. They are zones where faculty and students can feel free to pursue any idea, any line of argument, and any intellectual pursuit that they wish—free of the constraints of political pressure, cultural convention, or material interest. Closely related to this is the fact that universities become zones where play is not only permissible but even desirable, where it's OK to pursue an idea just because it's intriguing, even though there is no apparent practical benefit that this pursuit would produce.

This, of course, is a rather idealized version of the university. In practice, as we know, politics, convention, and economics constantly intrude on the zone of autonomy in an effort to shape the process and limit these freedoms. This is particularly true in the lower strata of the system. My argument is not that the ideal is met but that the structure of American higher education—especially in the top tiers of the system—creates a space of relative autonomy, where these constraining forces are partially held back, allowing the possibility for free intellectual pursuits that cannot be found anywhere else.

Free intellectual play is what we in the faculty tend to care about, but others in American society see other benefits arising from higher education that justify the enormous amount of public and private time and treasure that we devote to supporting the system. Policy makers and employers put primary emphasis on higher education as an engine of human capital production, which provides the economically relevant skills that drive increases in worker productivity and growth in the gross domestic product. They also hail it as a place of knowledge production, where people develop valuable technologies, theories, and inventions that can feed directly into the economy. And companies use it as a place to outsource many of their needs for workforce training and research and development.

These pragmatic benefits that people see coming from the system of higher education are real. Universities truly are socially useful in such ways. But it's important to keep in mind that these social benefits can only arise if the university remains a preserve for free intellectual play. Universities are much less useful to society if they restrict themselves to the training of individuals for particular present-day jobs or to the production of research to solve current problems. They are most useful if they function as storehouses for knowledges, skills, technologies, and theories—for which there is no current application but which may turn out to be enormously useful in the future. They are the mechanism by which modern societies build capacity to deal with issues that have not yet emerged but sooner or later are likely to do so.

A critical point about the American system of higher education that I want make in this book is that it is good for a lot of things but it was established in order to accomplish *none* of these things. As I have shown, the system that arose in the nineteenth century was not trying to store knowledge, produce capacity, or increase productivity. And it wasn't trying to promote free speech or encourage play with ideas. It wasn't even trying to preserve institutional autonomy. These things happened as the system developed, but they were all unintended consequences. What was driving development of the system was a clash of competing interests, all of which saw the college as a useful medium for meeting particular ends. Religious denominations saw them as a way to spread the faith. Town fathers saw them as a way to promote local development and increase property values. The federal government saw them as a way to spur the sale of federal lands. State governments saw them as a way to establish credibility in competition with other states. College presidents and faculty saw them as a way to promote their own careers. And at the base of the whole process of system development were the consumers, the students, without whose enrollment and tuition and donations and loyalty the system would not have been able to persist. The consumers saw the college as useful in a number of ways: as a medium for seeking social opportunity and achieving social mobility; as a medium for preserving social advantage and avoiding downward mobility; as a place to have a good time, enjoy an easy transition to adulthood, pick up some social skills, and meet a spouse; even, sometimes, as a place to learn.

The paradox is that the primary benefits of the system of higher education derive from its form, but this form did not arise in order to produce these benefits. We need to preserve the form in order to continue enjoying these benefits, but unfortunately the organizational foundations on which the form is built are, on the face of it, absurd. Central to these mechanisms is that the university protects the faculty from the real world, protects faculty from each other, and hides what we're doing behind a screen of fictions and veneers that keep anyone from knowing exactly what is really going on. Awkwardly, this means that the institution depends on attributes that reasonable people would find deplorable: organizational anarchy, professional hypocrisy, and public inscrutability.

Each of these foundational qualities is currently under attack from reformers whose alternative visions of higher education, unfortunately, have a certain face validity. If the attackers accomplish their goals, however, the system's form, which has been so enormously productive over the years, will collapse, and with this collapse will come the end of the university as we know it. I didn't promise this book would end well, did I?

Current Efforts to Remake the System in a More Reasonable Form

Let me spell out three challenges that would undercut the core autonomy and synergy that makes the system so productive in its current form. On the surface, each of the proposed changes seems quite sensible and desirable. Only by examining the implications of actually pursuing these changes can we see how they threaten the foundational qualities that currently undergird the system. Unfortunately, the system's foundations are so paradoxical that mounting a public defense of them is difficult indeed. Yet it is precisely these traits of the system that we need to defend in order to preserve the current highly functional form of the university. In what follows, I am drawing inspiration from the work of Suzanne Lohmann, a political scientist at UCLA, who is the scholar who has addressed these issues most directly.[5]

One challenge comes from prospective reformers of American higher education who want to promote *transparency*. Who can be against that? This idea derives from the accountability movement, which has already swept across elementary and secondary education and is now pounding on the shores of higher education. It simply asks universities to show people what they're doing. What is the university doing with its money and its effort? Who is paying for what? How do the various pieces of the complex structure of the university fit together? And are they self-supporting or drawing resources from elsewhere? What is faculty credit-hour production? How is tuition related to instructional costs? And so on. These demands make a lot of sense.

The problem, however, as I have shown, is that the autonomy of the university depends on its ability to shield its inner workings from public scrutiny. It relies on *opacity*. Autonomy will end if the public can see everything that is going on and what everything costs. Consider all the cross-subsidies that keep the institution afloat: undergraduates support graduate education, professional schools support the humanities, adjuncts subsidize professors, and rich schools subsidize poor schools. Consider all of the instructional activities that would wilt in the light of day; consider all of the research projects that could be seen as useless or politically unacceptable. The current structure keeps the inner workings of the system obscure, which protects the university from intrusions on its autonomy. Remember, this autonomy arose by accident not by design; its persistence depends on keeping the details of university operations out of public view.

A second and related challenge comes from reformers who seek to promote *disaggregation*. The university is an organizational nightmare, they say, with all of those institutes and centers, departments and schools, programs and administrative offices. There are no clear lines of authority, no mechanisms to promote efficiency and eliminate duplication, no tools to achieve economies of scale. Transparency is one step in the right direction, they say, but the real reform that is needed is to take apart the complex interdependencies and overlapping responsibilities within the university and then figure out how each of these tasks could be accomplished in the most cost-effective and outcome-effective manner. Why not have a few star professors tape lectures and then offer massive open online courses at colleges across the country? Why not have institutions specialize in what they're best at—remedial education, undergraduate instruction, vocational education, research production, or graduate student training? Putting them together into a single institution is expensive and grossly inefficient.

But recall that it is precisely the aggregation of purposes and functions—the combination of the populist, the practical, and the elite—that has made the university so strong, so successful, and, yes, so useful. This combination creates a strong base both financially and politically and allows for forms of synergy than cannot happen with a set of isolated educational functions. The fact is that this institution can't be disaggregated without losing what makes it the kind of university that students, policy makers, employers, and the general public find so compelling. A key organizational element that makes the university so effective is its *anarchic complexity*.

A third challenge comes not from reformers intruding on the university from the outside but from faculty members meddling with it from the inside. The threat here arises from the dangerous practice of acting on *academic principle*. Fortunately, this is not that common in academe. But the danger is lurking in the background of every decision about faculty hires. Here's how it works. You review a finalist for a faculty position in a field not closely connected to your own, and you find to your horror that the candidate's intellectual field seems absurd on the face of it (how can anyone take this type of work seriously?) and the candidate's own scholarship in the field doesn't seem credible. So you decide to speak against hiring the candidate and organize colleagues to support your position. Dangerous move.

Universities are structured in a manner that protects the faculty from the outside world (i.e., protecting them from the forces of transparency and disaggregation), but it's also organized in a manner that protects the faculty from each other. The latter is the reason we have such an enormous array of departments and schools in universities. If every historian had to meet the approval of geologists and every psychologist had be meet the approval of law faculty, no one would ever be hired.

The simple fact is that part of what keeps universities healthy and autonomous is *hypocrisy*. Because of the Balkanized structure of university organization (the department system), we all have our own protected spaces to operate in and we all pass judgment only on our own peers within that space. To do otherwise would be chaos. We don't have to respect each other's work across campus, we merely need to tolerate it. You pick your faculty, we'll pick ours. Lohmann calls this core procedure of the academy "logrolling."[6] In public we grant colleagues outside our own areas of specialization formal respect, but in private we scorn them. And that's a good thing. If we all operated on principle, if we all only approved scholars we respected, then the university would be a much diminished place. Put another way, I wouldn't want to belong to a university that consisted only of people I found worthy. Gone would be the diversity of views, paradigms, methodologies, theories, and worldviews that makes the university such a rich place. The result is incredibly messy, and it permits a lot of quirky—even ridiculous—research agendas, courses, and instructional programs. But in aggregate, this libertarian chaos includes an extraordinary range of ideas, capacities, theories, and social possibilities. It's exactly the kind of mess we need to treasure and preserve and defend from all opponents.

So here is the thought I'm leaving you with. The American system of higher education is enormously productive and useful, and it's a great resource for students, faculty, policy makers, employers, and society. What makes it work is not its substance but its form. The form makes no sense to outsiders but it's enormously effective. So we need to avoid the urge to remake it in a more rationalized form.

Of course, that will never happen. Higher ed is now in the crosshairs of educational policy reformers, since it has evolved into the central educational institution for allocating social opportunity and social advantage. It's in the uncomfortable position occupied by the high school for most of the twentieth century, and as a result it's the natural target for our worst fears and greatest aspirations. For anyone who wants to get ahead or stay ahead—and how many people really don't want one or the other?—it serves as the indispensable and inscrutable road map to the American Dream. And therefore it has become a problem that needs to be solved. Even if that would be best for everyone, leaving it alone is not an option. We feel the need to deploy the machinery of policy to diagnose its ailment and prescribe a cure. In short, we need a plan.

In my view, however, the problem with this prospect is that what has made the system so effective at what it does is precisely that *it arose without a plan*. It arose as a side effect of efforts by a variety of actors—land speculators, churches, and educational consumers—to pursue a variety of ends that had nothing to do with creating a system of higher education. They wanted to increase land value, promote the faith, and get a good job. They weren't trying to construct the current astonishingly complex and highly stratified structure of nearly 5,000 institutions, ranging from the inclusive community college to the exclusive research university. The system is something that just happened—an accident of accumulating unintended consequences.

Educational policy didn't make the system; the system made educational policy. The system's generating vision was of higher education as a private good, and for the last 100 years in particular this vision revolved around higher ed as the primary mechanism for passing on social privilege and pursuing social opportunity. Consumers voted with their feet, sending their children to college in ever-increasing numbers, and they also voted with ballots, electing political leaders who would meet this demand by continually expanding the system. Public policy for higher education followed on the heels of consumers pursuing higher education for private gain. For one brief period during the Cold War, the system took on a public role as savior of a nation, but it has since reverted to type, as a private good promoting individual interests. It continues to serve the public good—promoting economic growth, national power, cultural richness—but only as a side effect of its core dynamic, which is driven by private actors pursuing personal benefit.

In its current form, the system drives policy makers crazy. The problem is not just what I pointed out in the previous pages—that its workings are opaque, its accountability structure murky, and its organizational form befuddlingly complex. The central problem is that the system is wholly at odds with itself. At its core, it is riddled with contradictions. It just doesn't make sense. Or, more correctly, it makes sense in a wide variety of ways that seem to cancel each other out, leaving a muddle that begs to be cleared up. That's what the various plans for reform call for: disentangle; clarify; cut back to a central mission; separate functions; focus budgets around these missions and functions; cut costs. Ultimately the idea is to provide the consumer with a leaner, cheaper, more effective, and more focused array of higher education products.

What reformers don't acknowledge, however, is the uncomfortable fact that this ungainly system of higher education is in fact doing just what we want it to. It arose by being remarkably responsive to its environment, and its apparently dysfunctional structure was built through a process of meeting demand by accumulating multiple functions, cultivating multiple constituencies, and continually seeking out new sources of support. It has long offered something for everyone, so there's no way it was ever going to be lean and focused. Instead, it's messy—a reflection, or perhaps refraction, of the contradictory array of things we have asked it to be. It's the people's college, the party school, the scholar's retreat, the economic engine, the public park, the tower of learning, the training ground, the bulwark of privilege, the cultural repository, the public entertainer, the gateway to the middle class, the club, the colosseum, and the conservatory.

It's an organized anarchy, a perfect mess. The system responds with great vigor, and to great effect, to policies that aim to feed it rather than reform it. Recall the glory days of the Cold War, when a massive infusion of federal and state money turned a promising system of higher education into the envy of the world. But these days no one is talking about that kind of educational policy: a flood of funding with no strings attached. Now the formula is less funding and more strings. Restrict focus for each institution to a core function, cut everything else as frills and fluff, and hold the institution accountable for meeting its policy and financial targets. In short, do less with less. The result is to cut away the critical supports that made the system so effective—its autonomy, its flexibility, its consumer sensitivity, and its comprehensive complexity.

So let me leave you with one thought: Why ruin a perfect mess? In order to enjoy its benefits, we need to leave it alone.

ACKNOWLEDGMENTS

Like most of my earlier writing, this book emerged from my work as a teacher, in particular from teaching the class on the history of higher education in the United States at the Stanford University Graduate School of Education over the last decade. When I teach a class, I have to develop a story about the issues that surround the topic and that arise from the relevant literature. Then, after trying out the story for a while, I need to see if it has enough durability to put it on paper. Teaching allows the flexibility to develop an idea, but print is where the idea has to show its ability to survive critical scrutiny. As I tell my students, talking about ideas in the classroom is like singing in the shower; it may sound good there, but the real test comes in the recording studio. I hope this book survives that test.

I am grateful to a large number of colleagues for help in constructing this book. This includes colleagues from Stanford (David Tyack, Larry Cuban, Mitchell Stevens, Chiqui Ramirez, Leah Gordon, Dick Scott, Patti Gumport, and Ethan Ris); scholars from across the United States (Jeff Mirel, Tom Popkewitz, Nick Burbules, Lynn Fendler, H. D. Meyer, and Steven Brint); and another group of scholars in Europe (Daniel Tröhler, Marc Depaepe, Paul Smeyers, Fritz Osterwalder, and Jón Torfi Jónasson).

In the past few years I've been able to try out some of the ideas in this book at a variety of scholarly forums. These have included the annual meetings of the American Educational Research Association and the History of Education Society. They also included some more intimate settings, including the annual meetings of the Research Community on the Philosophy and History of the Discipline of Education; several conferences at Centro Stefano Franscini, Ascona, Switzerland; a conference on higher education at Peking University; and a series of annual meetings of the international Doctoral Conference on Theory and Data in the History of Education.

My editor at Chicago, Elizabeth Branch Dyson, has given me excellent advice and provided strong support for this project over the last several years. And I am grateful to the Stanford Graduate School of Education and Dean Deborah Stipek for the sabbatical that allowed me the time to complete the manuscript.

Finally, I am deeply grateful for the tolerance, love, and support that I received throughout the turbulent course of this book's evolution from my beloved wife, Diane Churchill, to whom this book is dedicated.

Some of the material in this book has appeared in print in an earlier form. I am grateful to the publishers for permission to reuse that material here.

"An Affair to Remember: America's Brief Fling with the University as a Public Good." *Journal of Philosophy of Education* 50, no. 1 (2016): 20–36. With permission of John Wiley and Sons.

"College—What Is It Good For?" *Education and Culture* 30, no. 1 (2014): 3–15. With permission of Purdue University Press.

"A System without a Plan: Emergence of an American System of Higher Education in the Twentieth Century." *Bildungsgeschichte: International Journal for the Historiography of Education* 3, no. 1 (2013): 46–59. With permission of Verlag Julius Klinkhardt.

"Balancing Access and Advantage in the History of American Schooling." In *Bildungsungleichheit und Gerechtigkeit: Wissenschaftliche und Gesellschaftliche Herausforderungen*, edited by Rolf Becker, Patrick Bühler, and Thomas Bühler, 101–14. Bern: Haupt Verlag, 2013. With permission of Haupt Verlag.

"The Power of the Parochial in Shaping the American System of Higher Education." In *Educational Research: The Importance and Effects of Institutional Spaces*, edited by Paul Smeyers and Marc Depaepe, 31–46. Dordrecht: Springer, 2013. With permission of Springer.

"Mutual Subversion: A Short History of the Liberal and the Professional in American Higher Education." *History of Education Quarterly* 46, no. 1 (2006): 1–15. With permission of John Wiley and Sons.

NOTES

Chapter One

1. What I'm calling colleges and universities are postsecondary institutions that grant degrees, of which there are about 4,700. There an additional 2,500 institutions that don't grant degrees, primarily vocational schools for fields such as cosmetology and truck driving. National Center for Education Statistics (NCES]2014]), table 105.50.
2. Clark 1983.
3. Kerr 2001, 115.
4. Institute of Higher Education 2014.
5. *Times Higher Education Supplement* 2015.
6. Webometrics Ranking of World Universities 2014.
7. Fisher 2013.
8. Bothwell 2015; "Nobel Prize Facts" 2015.
9. Hartz 1955, 3.
10. Trow 1988, 1999.
11. Trow 1988, 15.
12. Pew Charitable Trusts 2015, fig. 8.
13. NCES 1993, fig. 20; 2002, figs. 18 and 19.
14. *Chronicle of Higher Education* 2014a.
15. *U.S. News and World Report* 2012.
16. Riesman 1958.
17. Geiger 2004a, 270.
18. Kerr 2001, 7–14.
19. *Princeton Review* 2014.
20. Pedersen 1997.
21. Clark 2006.
22. Weber 1978, 215–16.
23. Ibid., 215.

24. Lodge 1979, 1995; Bradbury 1985, 2000.
25. The American university's mixed sources of authority align with the characterization of this institution by Michael Cohen and James March (1974, 3) as the "prototypic organized anarchy." In their view, university presidents have to deal with unresolvable ambiguity in four major areas: purpose, power, experience, and success (195).
26. Burton Clark (1983) argues that a central strength of the American system of higher education is structural complexity, with radical decentralization and a federalized dispersion of power.

Chapter Two

1. Boorstin 1965; Potts 1971; Brown 1995.
2. Tewksbury 1965, table 1; Collins 1979, table 5.2.
3. Rüegg 2004.
4. Burke 1982, 67.
5. Ibid., computed from tables 1.5 and 2.2.
6. Carter et al. 2006, table Bc523.
7. Ibid., table Bc571.
8. U.S. Bureau of the Census 1975, ser. H 751.
9. Burke 1982, table 1.9.
10. Kelly 2015.
11. Quoted in Boorstin (1965), 154.
12. Boorstin (1965) referred to the phenomenon of "the booster college."
13. Quoted in Brown (1995), 89.
14. Brown 1995, 93.
15. Benjamin Labaree was my grandfather's grandfather.
16. Middlebury Alumni Association 1975, 20.
17. Ibid.
18. Tewksbury 1965, tables 12 and 13.
19. Quoted in Thelin 2004b, 90.
20. In one extreme case, New York did not establish a state university until 1948.
21. Tewksbury 1965, 187.
22. National Research Council 1995, table 1.1.
23. Ogren (2005), calculated from app., 370–90.
24. Ogren 2005, app.
25. Collins 1979, table 5.2.
26. Burke 1982, table 1.2. Tewksbury (1965, table 2) argued that the failure rate on the frontier was much higher than this. He calculated that, in sixteen states outside of New England between 1800 and 1860, the college mortality rate was an astonishing 81 percent. Burke (1982, 13), however, says that this estimate is much too high, because Tewksbury counted a college as being founded if it received a state charter. But many of these chartered institutions never opened their doors, and many were high-school-level academies rather than colleges. All of this confusion about what was a college and what was a failure underscores the fluidity and volatility of the situation facing American colleges in this period.

27.   Kerr 2001, 14.
28.   Hofstadter 1962.

Chapter Three

1.   Quoted in Rudolph (1962), 220.
2.   Quoted in ibid., 238.
3.   Burke 1982, 154, 186, table 4.5.
4.   Carter et al. 2006, table Bc523.
5.   Rudolph 1962.
6.   Geiger 2004a, 270.
7.   On funding from private donations and foundations, see Geiger (2004a), 77–93.
8.   Barrow (1990), tables 2.1 and 2.2. These samples include both colleges and research universities.
9.   U.S. Bureau of the Census 1975, H 709.
10.   Flexner 1930, 45.
11.   Kerr 1968, xvii.
12.   Johnson 1978; Sellers 1991.
13.   Bledstein 1976, x.
14.   Ibid., 86; Kett 1977, 154.
15.   Bledstein 1976, 123.
16.   For census data on average years of schooling, see NCES (1993), table 5.
17.   We'll examine this process in more detail in chapter 5.
18.   Collins 1979, table 5.2.
19.   Camp 1915, 296–304.
20.   Quoted in Ris (2014).
21.   Brown 1995, chap. 6.
22.   Ris 2016.
23.   Thelin 2004b, 163.

Chapter Four

1.   Flexner 1930.
2.   Grubb and Lazerson 2004.
3.   Veysey 1970.
4.   Kerr 2001, 7–14.
5.   Goodwin 1973, 157.
6.   Levine 1986, 68.
7.   Ibid., 40.
8.   Ibid., 135.
9.   Ibid., 40.
10.   Ibid., 90–97.
11.   Brint (2002), 235; italics removed from the original.
12.   Ibid.
13.   Brubacher and Rudy 1997.

14.   Hughes and DeBaggis 1973.
15.   Thorne 1973; Amsterdan 1984.
16.   Goodlad 1990, 247.
17.   Schlossman et al. 1987; Schlossman and Sedlak 1988; Schlossman et al. 1994.
18.   Brint 2002, 251.
19.   There is a parallel in secondary education as well. As Angus and Mirel (1999) have shown, vocational courses at the high school level never constituted more than 10 percent of course taking, and a lot of those courses were general education under vocational labels (business English, business math).
20.   Levine 1986, 60.
21.   Turner 1960.
22.   Abbott 2002; Brint 2002; Chait 2002.
23.   Ben-David 1972, 43
24.   The Morrill Act 1862 (12 U.S. Statutes at Large, 503–505), section 4.
25.   For example, there are Michigan and Michigan State, Texas and Texas A & M. An exception that proves the rule is Ohio State, whose official name is The Ohio State University, in order to distinguish itself from the older private institution named Ohio University and also show that the "State" label should not lead anyone to assume it is not the flagship institution.
26.   Rudolph (1962, 467) notes that some 160 normal schools ended up becoming community colleges.
27.   Brint and Karabel 1989; Labaree 1997, chap. 8.
28.   I am grateful to Jeffrey Mirel for reminding me of the major role community colleges play in liberal arts instruction.
29.   Carter et al. 2006, tables Bc510–522 and Bc524.
30.   The 34 percent figure is for recent high school grads in 2013 (NCES [2015a], table 302.30). For the percentage for 1900, see Carter et al. (2006), table Bc524, measuring the proportion of population attending college at ages eighteen to twenty-four.
31.   Ben-David 1972, 44.
32.   Ibid.
33.   Veysey 1970; Brown 1995; Levine 1986; Dunham 1969; Brint and Karabel 1989; Brint 2002; and Geiger 2004a.
34.   Veysey 1970, 440.

Chapter Five

1.   Beck 2007. See also Gellert 1996 and Goldthorpe 1996.
2.   Simon 1973.
3.   For an extended discussion of the creation of universal schooling in the United States, see chap. 2 in Labaree (2010).
4.   For a more detailed account of the founding of Central High School, see chap. 2 in Labaree (1988).
5.   Katz 1968, pt. 1, chap. 1.
6.   Goldin and Katz 2008, 19.
7.   U.S. Bureau of the Census 1975, table H-424.

8.   Ibid.
9.   U.S. Dept. of Education 1993, table 9.
10.   Ibid., table 24.
11.   Levine 1986.
12.   U.S. Dept. of Education 1993, table 23.
13.   Ibid., table 24.
14.   Cahalan and Perna 2015, 30–31.
15.   Ibid., 32–33.

Chapter Six

1.   Institute of Higher Education 2014.
2.   NCES 2014, table 303.10.
3.   Thelin 2004a, 29.
4.   Thelin 1982, 88.
5.   Quoted in Rudolph (1962), 185; inflation calculation from Morgan Friedman, "The Inflation Calculator," http://www.westegg.com/inflation/index.html.
6.   Rudolph (1962), 185–86; inflation calculation from Friedman, "The Inflation Calculator.".
7.   Ben-David 1972, 33.
8.   Rudolph 1962, 189.
9.   Quoted in Kimball and Johnson 2012, 224.
10.   Kimball and Johnson 2012, 225.
11.   I ran into the sentiment again recently, quoted on the first page of Thelin's *A History of American Higher Education* (2004b), xiii, drawn from a 1963 Harvard brochure.
12.   Carter et al. 2006, table Bc510–522.
13.   NCES 2014, table 317.10.
14.   Thelin 1982, 87–88.
15.   Carter et al. 2006, table bc510–522.
16.   NCES 2014, table 303.10.
17.   In the more elaborated classification system used by the Carnegie Classification of Institutions of Higher Education (2016), the equivalent tiers are their top three classifications assigned to institutions that offer doctoral degrees: highest research activity, higher research activity, and moderate research activity.
18.   University of California Office of the President 2015, table 2.
19.   *U.S. News and World Report* 2015d.
20.   *U.S. News and World Report* 2015b.
21.   *U.S. News and World Report* 2015c.
22.   Avery et al. 2004, table 3.
23.   Stanford University 2015.
24.   UC Berkeley 2015.
25.   *U.S. News and World Report* 2015a.
26.   Burris 2004.
27.   Zumeta 2004, 85.

28. Aghion et al. 2010, 12.
29. Korn 2015.
30. Boston College (2014); drawn from the 2014 NACUBO-Commonfund Study of Endowments.
31. *Chronicle of Higher Education* (2014b). I'm leaving out the money raised by two large university systems, Texas and California.
32. Mora and Nugent 1998, 114.
33. Institute of Higher Education 2014.
34. *Chronicle of Higher Education* 2015.
35. Alexander 2001, fig. 1.
36. Riggs 2011.
37. Karabel 2005, 252–53; Bender 1961.
38. Bender 1961, 24, emphasis in original.
39. Kerr 2001, 1.
40. Money 2015.
41. Pell Institute and Pennahead 2015, 17.
42. Lewin 2015.
43. Aghion et al. 2010, 2.
44. Ibid., 10–11.
45. Quoted in Martinez and Nodine (1997), 167n11.
46. Institute of Higher Education 2014.
47. Ibid.
48. Warrell and Authers 2014; ETH Zurich 2014; *Chronicle of Higher Education* 2014b; Boston College 2014.
49. Dunham 1969, 25.
50. Shils (1973), 8, drawing on Cartter (1966).
51. Burris 2004.
52. *U.S. News and World Report* 2015a.
53. California State University 2015.
54. Institute of Higher Education 2014.

Chapter Seven

1. Carter et al. 2006, table Bc523.
2. Ibid., tables Bc510 to Bc520.
3. Terkel 1997.
4. Garrett and Rhine 2006, fig. 3.
5. Levine (1986), 51. Under pressure of the war effort, the department eventually relented and enlisted the help of chemists to study gas warfare. But the initial response is telling.
6. Geiger 2004b, 40–41; Carter et al. 2006, table Bc523.
7. Loss 2011.
8. American Association for the Advancement of Science (2015). Not all of this funding went into the higher education system. Some went to stand-alone research organizations such as the Rand Corporation and American Institute of Research. But these organizations in many ways function as an adjunct to

higher education, with researchers moving freely between them and the university.

9. American Association for the Advancement of Science 2015.
10. Carter et al. 2006, table Bc523; NCES 2014, table 303.10.
11. President's Commission, 1947, 1:6.
12. Ibid., 1:36
13. Carter et al. (2006), table Bc523; Douglass (2000), table 1; community college data for 1972 from Brossman (1973).
14. Martin 2008.
15. UC Data Analysis (2014), "State Funding for UC per Undergraduate Student."
16. Ibid., "Average UC Undergraduate Resident 'Fees.'"
17. State Higher Education Executive Officers 2013, fig. 3.
18. Pell Institute and Pennahead 2015, 25.
19. National Science Board 2012, fig. 5.
20. University of Virginia 2014.
21. Pell Institute and Pennahead 2015, 20.
22. McPherson and Schapiro 1998, table 3.3; College Board 2013, table 1.
23. College Board 2014, table 1.
24. American Association for the Advancement of Science 2015.
25. NCES 2014, table 303.10; American Association for the Advancement of Science 2015; College Board 2014, table 1.
26. Mortenson 2012.
27. Organisation for Economic Co-operation and Development 2012, 7.
28. Ibid., 8.
29. Ibid., 4.

Chapter Eight

1. The selectivity measures are developed by Barron's (Center for Public Education 2015). I calculated this number from a table using Barron's data showing the three highest categories, which accept more than 50 percent (Leonhardt, 2013).
2. Hess and Gift 2009.
3. American Association of Universities 2014.
4. Wai 2013.
5. Oremus 2014.
6. See California State University 2015; and Carson 2015, respectively.
7. California State University 2015.
8. Pell Institute and Pennahead 2015, 31.
9. Ibid.
10. NCES 2014, table 326.20; and Community College Research Center 2015, respectively.
11. Pew Charitable Trusts Economic Mobility Project 2012, fig. 3.
12. Karabel 2005, 547.
13. NCES 2014, table 301.10.
14. American Association of Universities (2015); Carnegie Classification of Insti-

tutions of Higher Education (2016). Carnegie labels these institutions doctoral universities—highest research activity.

15. Burris 2004.
16. Nerad, Aanerud, and Cerny 1999.
17. NCES 2014, table 315.50.
18. NCES 2015b, table 5.
19. Weissmann 2013.
20. Carnegie Classification of Institutions of Higher Education 2010.

Chapter Nine

1. On the rising number of graduate degrees, see NCES, 2014, table 301.10.
2. An additional 7 percent attend liberal arts colleges and 3 percent attend special purpose institutions in fields like art and theology. These data are for 2009, including public, private, and for-profit institutions. Carnegie Classification of Institutions of Higher Education (2011).
3. Cohen, March, and Olsen 1972, 1.
4. Carlin 1999.
5. Lohmann 2004, 2006.
6. Lohmann 2006.

REFERENCES

Abbott, Andrew. 2002. "The Disciplines and the Future." In *The Future of the City of Intellect: The Changing American University*, edited by Steven Brint, 205–30. Stanford, CA: Stanford University Press.

Aghion, Philippe, Mathias Dewatripont, Caroline Hoxby, Andreu Mas-Colell, and Andru Sapir. 2010. "The Governance and Performance of Universities: Evidence from Europe and the US." *Economic Policy* 25 (61): 7–59.

Alexander, F. King. 2001. "The Silent Crisis: The Relative Fiscal Capacity of Public Universities to Compete for Faculty." *Review of Higher Education* 24 (2): 113–29.

American Association for the Advancement of Science. 2015. "Federal Spending on Defense and NonDefense R&D." Last updated May 2015. http://www.aaas.org/sites/default/files/Function_1.jpg.

American Association of Universities. 2015. "AAU by the Numbers." Compiled August 2015. https://www.aau.edu/WorkArea/DownloadAsset.aspx?id=13460.

Amsterdan, Anthony G. 1984. "Clinical Legal Education—a 21st Century Perspective." *Journal of Legal Education* 34 (4): 612–18.

Angus, David, and Jeffrey Mirel. 1999. *The Failed Promise of the American High School, 1890–1995*. New York: Teachers College Press.

Avery, Christopher, Mark Glickman, Caroline Hoxby, and Andrew Metrick. 2004. "A Revealed Preference Ranking of U.S. Colleges and Universities." NBER Working Paper 10803. National Bureau of Economic Research, Cambridge, MA.

Barrow, Clyde W. 1990. *Universities and the Capitalist State: Corporate Liberalism and the Reconstruction of American Higher Education, 1894–1928*. Madison, University of Wisconsin Press.

Beck, Ulrich. 2007. "Beyond Class and Nation: Reframing Social Inequalities in a Globalizing World." *British Journal of Sociology* 58 (4): 680–705.

Ben-David, Joseph. 1972. *American Higher Education: Directions Old and New*. New York: McGraw-Hill.

Bender, Wilbur J. 1961. "The Top-One-Percent Policy: A Hard Look at the Dangers of an Academically Elite Harvard." *Harvard Alumni Bulletin*, vol. 30 (September).

Bledstein, Burton J. 1976. *The Culture of Professionalism: The Middle Class and the Development of Higher Education in America*. New York: W. W. Norton.

Boorstin, Daniel J. 1965. "Culture with Many Capitals: The Booster College." In *The Americans: The National Experience*, 152–61. New York: Knopf Doubleday.

Boston College. 2014. "Top 50 Endowments." Last updated March 11. http://www-test.bc.edu/offices/endowment/top50endowments.html.

Bothwell, Ellie. 2015. "Stanford Top University for Producing Nobel Prizes." *Times Higher Education* (August 6). https://www.timeshighereducation.co.uk/news/stanford-top-university-for-producing-nobel-laureates.

Bradbury, Malcolm. 1985. *The History Man*. London: Penguin.

———. 2000. *To the Hermitage*. New York: Overlook Press.

Brint, Steven. 2002. "The Rise of the 'Practical Arts.'" In *The Future of the City of Intellect: The Changing American University*, edited by Steven Brint, 231–59. Stanford, CA: Stanford University Press.

Brint, Steven, and Jerome Karabel. 1989. *The Diverted Dream: Community Colleges and the Promise of Educational Opportunity in America, 1900–1985*. New York: Oxford University Press.

Brossman, Sidney W. 1973. *The California Community Colleges*. Palo Alto, CA: Field Educational Publications.

Brown, David K. 1995. *Degrees of Control: A Sociology of Educational Expansion and Occupational Credentialism*. New York: Teachers College Press.

Brubacher, John S., and Willis Rudy. 1997. "Professional Education." In *ASHE Reader on the History of Higher Education*, edited by Lester F. Goodchild, and Harold S. Wechsler, 379–93. 2nd ed. Boston: Pearson Custom Publishing.

Burke, Colin B. 1982. *American Collegiate Populations: A Test of the Traditional View*. New York: New York University Press.

Burris, Val. 2004. "The Academic Caste System: Prestige Hierarchies in PhD Exchange Networks." *American Sociological Review* 69:239–64.

Cahalan, Margaret, and Laura Perna. 2015. *Indicators of Higher Education Equity in the United States: 45 Year Trend Report 2015*. Philadelphia: Penn Ahead Alliance for Higher Education and Democracy; Pell Institute for the Study of Opportunity in Higher Educaton.

California State University. 2015. "CSU New Students (Duplicated) Applications and Admission by Campus and Student Level, Fall 2014. April 15. http://www.calstate.edu/AS/stat_reports/2014–2015/apps_f2014_all.htm.

Camp, Walter, ed. 1915. *Spalding's Official Foot Ball Guide, 1915*. New York: American Sports Publishing.

Carlin, James F. 1999. "Restoring Sanity to an Academic World Gone Mad." *Chronicle of Higher Education*. November 5. http://chronicle.com/article/Restoring-Sanity-to-an/20125/.

Carnegie Classification of Institutions of Higher Education. 2016. Basic Classification Description. Accessed June 4, 2016. http://carnegieclassifications.iu.edu/summary/basic.php.

———. 2015. Carnegie Classifications Data File. Accessed July 27, 2015. http://carnegie classifications.iu.edu/resources/.

———. 2010. 2010 Data File. Accessed July 29, 2015. http://carnegieclassifications.iu.edu/downloads.php.

Carson, Biz. 2015. "The 20 Universities That Are Most Likely to Land You a Job in Silicon Valley." *Business Insider*. July 13. http://www.businessinsider.com/silicon -valley-hiring-most-popular-universities-2015-7.

Carter, Susan B., et al. 2006. *Historical Statistics of the United States, Millennial Education on Line*. New York: Cambridge University Press.

Cartter, Alan M. 1966. *An Assessment of Quality in Graduate Education*. Washington, DC: American Council on Education.

Center for Public Education. 2015. "What Do You Mean by a 'Competitive' College?" January 15. http://www.centerforpubliceducation.org/Main-Menu /Staffingstudents/Chasing-the-college-acceptance-letter-Is-it-harder-to-get-into -college-At-a-glance/What-do-you-mean-by-a-competitive-college.html.

Chait, Richard. 2002. "The 'Academic Revolution' Revisited." In *The Future of the City of Intellect: The Changing American University*, edited by Steven Brint, 293–321. Stanford, CA: Stanford University Press.

Chronicle of Higher Education. 2015. "2013–14 Faculty Salary Survey." Accessed May 3, 2015. http://chronicle.com/article/2013-14-AAUP-Faculty-Salary/145679#id=table.

———. 2014a. "Who Pays for Public Higher Education." March 3. http://chronicle .com/article/Who-Pays-More/145063.

———. 2014b. "Money Raised by Colleges, 2013 Fiscal Year." February 12. http:// chronicle.com/article/Money-Raised-by-Colleges-2013/144689/.

Clark, Burton R. 1983. *The Higher Education System: Academic Organization in Cross-National Perspective*. Berkeley: University of California Press.

Clark, William. 2006. *Academic Charisma and the Origins of the Research University*. Chicago: University of Chicago Press.

Cohen, Michael D., and James G. March. 1974. *Leadership and Ambiguity*. 2nd ed. Boston: Harvard Business School Press.

Cohen, Michael D., James G. March, and Johan P. Olsen. 1972. "A Garbage Can Model of Organizational Choice." *Administrative Science Quarterly* 17 (1): 1–25.

College Board. 2013. *Trends in Student Aid, 2013*. New York: College Board.

———. 2014. "Trends in Higher Education: Total Federal and Nonfederal Loans over Time." Accessed September 4, 2014. https://trends.collegeboard.org/student-aid /figures-tables/growth-federal-and-nonfederal-loans-over-time.

Collins, Randall. 1979. *The Credential Society: An Historical Sociology of Education and Stratification*. New York: Academic Press.

Community College Research Center. 2015. "Community College FAQs." Teachers College, Columbia University. Accessed August 3, 2015. http://ccrc.tc.columbia .edu/Community-College-FAQs.html.

Douglass, John Aubrey. 2000. *The California Idea and American Higher Education: 1850 to the 1960 Master Plan*. Stanford, CA: Stanford University Press.

Dunham, Edgar Alden. 1969. *Colleges of the Forgotten Americans: A Profile of State Colleges and Universities*. New York: McGraw Hill.

ETH Zurich. 2014. "ETH Zurich in Figures." Accessed May 5, 2016. https://www.ethz .ch/en/the-eth-zurich/portrait/ETH%20Zurich%20in%20figures.html.

Fisher, Max. 2013. "The Amazing History of the Nobel Prize, Told in Maps and Charts." *Washington Post*. October 15. https://www.washingtonpost.com/news /worldviews/wp/2013/10/15/the-amazing-history-of-the-nobel-prize-told-in -maps-and-charts/.

Flexner, Abraham. 1930. *Universities: American, English, German.* New York: Oxford University Press.

Hofstadter, Richard. 1962. *Anti-Intellectualism in American Life.* New York: Vintage.

Garrett, Thomas A., and Russell M. Rhine. 2006. "On the Size and Growth of Government." *Federal Reserve Bank of St. Louis Review* 88 (1): 13–30.

Geiger, Roger L.2004a. *To Advance Knowledge: The Growth of American Research Universities, 1900–1940.* New Brunswick, NJ: Transaction.

———. 2004b. *Research and Relevant Knowledge: American Research Universities since World War II.* New Brunswick, NJ: Transaction.

Gellert, Claudius. 1996. "Recent Trends in German Higher Education." *European Journal of Education* 31 (3): 311–19.

Goldin, Claudia, and Lawrence F. Katz. 2008. *The Race between Education and Technology.* Cambridge, MA: Belknap Press of Harvard University Press.

Goldthorpe, John H. 1996. "Class Analysis and the Reorientation of Class Theory: The Case of Persisting Differentials in Educational Attainment." *British Journal of Sociology* 47 (3): 481–505.

Goodlad, John I. 1990. *Teachers for Our Nation's Schools.* San Francisco: Jossey-Bass.

Goodwin, Gregory L. 1973. *A Social Panacea: A History of the Community-Junior College Ideology.* ERIC document ED 093-427. Washington, DC: Educational Resources Information Center.

Grubb, W. Norton, and Marvin Lazerson. 2004. *The Education Gospel: The Economic Power of Schooling.* Cambridge, MA: Harvard University Press.

Hartz, Louis. 1955. *The Liberal Tradition in America.* New York: Harcourt, Brace & World.

Hess, Rick, and Thomas Gift. 2009. "Grade Inflation and Multiple Applications Can Make Schools Look Deceptively Good." *National Review.* March 23. http://www.nationalreview.com/article/227077/beware-college-rankings-frederick-m-hess-thomas-gift.

Hofstadter, Richard. 1962. *Anti-Intellectualism in American Life.* New York: Vintage.

Hughes, Everett C., and Agostino M. DeBaggis. 1973. "Systems of Theological Education in the United States." In *Education for the Professions of Medicine, Law, Theology, and Social Welfare,* edited by Everett C. Hughes, Barrie Thorne, Agostino M. DeBaggis, Arnold Gurin, and David Williams, 169–200. New York: McGraw-Hill.

Institute of Higher Education, Shanghai Jiao Tong University. 2014. "Academic Ranking of World Universities—2014." Accessed May 3, 2015. http://www.shanghairanking.com/ARWU2014.html.

Johnson, Paul E. 1978. *A Shopkeeper's Millennium: Society and Revivals in Rochester, New York, 1815–1837.* New York: Hill and Wang.

Karabel, Jerome. 2005. *The Chosen: The Hidden History of Admission and Exclusion at Harvard, Yale, and Princeton.* New York: Mariner Books.

Katz, Michael B. 1968. *The Irony of Early School Reform: Educational Innovation in Mid-Nineteenth Century Massachusetts.* Boston: Beacon Press.

Kelly, Matthew. 2015. The (District) Lines Are Drawn: Inequality and Shifting Meanings of Education in Nineteenth-Century California. Unpublished paper.

Kerr, Clark. 1968. "Introduction to the Transaction Edition: Remembering Flexner." In *Universities: American, English, German,* vii–xxx. New York: Oxford University Press.

———. 2001. *The Uses of the University*. 5th ed. Cambridge, MA: Harvard University Press.

Kett, Joseph F. 1977. *Rites of Passage*. New York: Basic.

Kimball, Bruce A., and Benjamin Ashby Johnson. 2012. "The Beginning of 'Free Money' Ideology in American Universities: Charles W. Eliot at Harvard, 1869–1909." *History of Education Quarterly* 52 (2): 222–50.

Korn, Melissa. 2015. "For U.S. Universities, the Rich Get Richer Faster." *Wall Street Journal*. April 16. http://www.wsj.com/articles/for-u-s-universities-the-rich-get-richer-faster-1429156904.

Labaree, David F. 1988. *The Making of an American High School: The Credentials Market and the Central High School of Philadelphia, 1838–1920*. New Haven, CT: Yale University Press.

———. 1997. *How to Succeed in School without Really Learning: The Credentials Race in American Education*. New Haven, CT: Yale University Press.

———. 2010. *Someone Has to Fail: The Zero-Sum Game of Public Schooling*. Cambridge, MA: Harvard University Press.

Leonhardt, David. 2013. "What Makes a College 'Selective'—and Why It Matters." *Economix* (blog). *New York Times*. April 4. http://economix.blogs.nytimes.com/2013/04/04/what-makes-a-college-selective-and-why-it-matters/.

Levine, David O. 1986. *The American College and the Culture of Aspiration, 1914–1940*. Ithaca, NY: Cornell University Press.

Lewin, Tamar. 2015. "For-Profit Colleges File for Bankruptcy." *New York Times*. May 4. http://www.nytimes.com/2015/05/05/education/for-profit-corinthian-colleges-file-for-bankruptcy.html.

Lodge, David. 1979. *Changing Places*. London: Penguin.

———. 1995. *Small World*. London: Penguin.

Lohmann, Susanne. 2004. "Darwinian Medicine for the University." In *Governing Academia*, edited by Ronald G. Ehrenberg, 71–90. Ithaca, NY: Cornell University Press.

———. 2006. "The Public Research University as a Complex Adaptive System." Unpublished manuscript, University of California, Los Angeles.

Loss, Christopher P. 2011. *Between Citizens and the State: The Politics of American Higher Education in the 20ᵗʰ Century*. Princeton, NJ: Princeton University Press.

Martin, Isaac William. 2008. *The Permanent Tax Revolt: How the Property Tax Transformed American Politics*. Stanford, CA: Stanford University Press.

Martinez, Mario C., and Thad Nodine. 1997. "Michigan: Fiscal Stability and Constitutional Autonomy." In *Public and Private Financing of Higher Education: Shaping Public Policy for the Future*, edited by Patrick M. Callan and Joni E. Finney, 137–68. Phoenix: American Council on Education and Oryx Press.

McPherson, Michael S., and Morton O. Schapiro. 1998. *The Student Aid Game: Meeting Need and Rewarding Talent in American Higher Education*. Princeton, NJ: Princeton University Press.

Middlebury Alumni Association. 1975. "Labaree Picks up the Pieces." In *Middlebury's 175 Anniversary*, 18–23. Middlebury VT: Alumni Association.

Money. 2015. "Money's Best Colleges." July. https://best-colleges.time.com/money/full-ranking#/list.

Mora, José-Ginés, and Michael Nugent. 1998. "Seeking New Resources for European

Universities: The Example of Fund-Raising in the US." *European Journal of Education* 33 (1): 113–29.

Mortenson, Thomas G. 2012. "State Funding: A Race to the Bottom." *The Presidency.* Winter. http://www.acenet.edu/the-presidency/columns-and-features/Pages/state -funding-a-race-to-the-bottom.aspx.

National Center for Education Statistics. 1993. *120 Years of American Education: A Statistical Portrait.* Washington, DC: Government Printing Office.

———. 2002. *Digest of Education Statistics, 2001.* Washington, DC: Government Printing Office.

———. 2014. *Digest of Education Statistics, 2013.* Washington, DC: Government Printing Office.

———. 2015a. "Most Current Digest Tables." Accessed August 7, 2015. http://nces.ed .gov/programs/digest/current_tables.asp.

———. 2015b. "Table 5: Number and Percentage of Instructional Staff at Title IV Degree-Granting Institutions Other Than Medical Schools, by Sector of Institution and Employment Status: United States, Fall 2003, 2005, 2007, and 2009." Accessed August 1, 2015. http://nces.ed.gov/datalab/tableslibrary/viewtable.aspx ?tableid=7093.

National Research Council. 1995. *Colleges of Agriculture at the Land Grant Universities: A Profile.* Washington, DC: National Academy Press.

National Science Board. 2012. *Diminishing Funding Expectations: Trends and Challenges for Public Research Universities.* Arlington, VA: National Science Foundation.

Nerad, Maresi, Rebecca Aanerud, and Joseph Cerny. 1999. "'So You Want to Become a Professor!' Lessons from the PhDs-Ten Years Later Study." In *Paths to the Professoriate: Strategies for Enriching the Preparation of Future Faculty,* edited by Donald H. Wulff, Ann E. Austin, and Associates, 137–58. San Francisco: Jossey-Bass.

"Nobel Prize Facts." 2015. Nobelprize.org. Accessed August 6, 2015. http://www .nobelprize.org/nobel_prizes/facts/.

Ogren, Christine. 2005. *The American State Normal School: "An Instrument of Great Good."* New York: Palgrave Macmillan.

Oremus, Will. 2014. "Where Do Googlers Go to College? A Look at Tech Companies' Top Feeder Schools." *Future Tense* (blog). *Slate.* May 23. http://www.slate .com/blogs/future_tense/2014/05/23/tech_company_feeder_schools_stanford_to _google_washington_to_microsoft_sjsu.html.

Organisation for Economic Co-operation and Development. 2012. "Education at a Glance: OECD Indicators 2012, United States." Accessed May 13, 2015. http://www .oecd.org/edu/CN%20-%20United%20States.pdf .

Pedersen, Olaf. 1997. *The First Universities: Studium Generale and the Origins of University Education in Europe.* Cambridge: Cambridge University Press.

Pell Institute and Pennahead. 2015. *Indicators of Higher Education Equity in the United States.* 2015 rev. ed. Philadelphia: Pell Institute for the Study of Opportunity in Higher Education and the University of Pennsylvania Alliance for Higher Education and Democracy (PennAHEAD). http://www.pellinstitute.org/publications -Indicators_of_Higher_Education_Equity_in_the_United_States_45_Year _Report.shtml.

Pew Charitable Trusts. 2015. "Federal and State Funding of Higher Education." Issue

Brief, June 11. http://www.pewtrusts.org/en/research-and-analysis/issue-briefs/2015/06/federal-and-state-funding-of-higher-education.

Pew Charitable Trusts Economic Mobility Project. 2012. *Pursuing the American Dream: Economic Mobility Across Generations*. Washington, DC: Pew Charitable Trusts. http://www.pewtrusts.org/en/research-and-analysis/reports/0001/01/01/pursuing-the-american-dream.

Potts, David B. 1971. "American Colleges in the Nineteenth Century: From Localism to Denominationalism." *History of Education Quarterly* 11 (4): 363–80.

President's Commission on Higher Education. 1947. *Higher Education for American Democracy: A Report*. Washington, DC: Government Printing Office.

Princeton Review. 2014. "Party Schools." Accessed July 10, 2014. http://www.princetonreview.com/schoolList.aspx?id=737.

Riesman, David. 1958. "The Academic Procession." In *Constraint and Variety in American Education*. Garden City, NY: Doubleday.

Riggs, Henry E. 2011. "The Price of Perception." *New York Times*. April 13. http://www.nytimes.com/2011/04/17/education/edlife/edl-17notebook-t.html.

Ris, Ethan W. 2014. "The Education of Andrew Carnegie: Strategic Philanthropy and Higher Education, 1880–1919." Paper presented at the American Educational Research Association Annual Meeting, Philadelphia, PA, April 3–7.

———. 2016. "Hierarchy as a Theme in the US College, 1880–1920." *History of Education* 45 (1): 57–78.

Rudolph, Frederick. 1962. *The American College and University: A History*. New York: Vintage.

Rüegg, Walter. 2004. "European Universities and Similar Institutions in Existence between 1812 and the End of 1944: A Chronological List: Universities." In *A History of the University in Europe*, vol. 3. London: Cambridge University Press.

Schlossman, Steven, Robert E. Gleeson, Michael Sedlak, and David Grayson Allen. 1994. *The Beginnings of Graduate Management Education in the United States*. Santa Monica, CA: Graduate Management Admission Council.

Schlossman, Steven, and Michael Sedlak. 1988. *The Age of Reform in American Management Education*. Santa Monica, CA: Graduate Management Admission Council.

Schlossman, Steven, Michael Sedlak, and Harold Wechsler. 1987. *The "New Look:" The Ford Foundation and the Revolution in Business Education*. Santa Monica, CA: Graduate Management Admission Council.

Sellers, Charles. 1991. *The Market Revolution: Jacksonian America, 1815–1846*. New York: Oxford University Press.

Shils, Edward. 1973. "The American Private University." *Minerva* 11:6–29.

Simon, P. 1973. "One Man's Ceiling Is Another Man's Floor." On *There Goes Rhymin' Simon*. Columbia Records, New York.

Stanford University. 2015. "Common Data Set 2014–2015." Stanford University Communications. Accessed April 29, 2015. http://ucomm.stanford.edu/cds/2014.

State Higher Education Executive Officers (SHEEO). 2013. *State Higher Education Finance, FY 2012*. www.sheeo.org/sites/default/files/publications/SHEF-FY12.pdf.

Terkel, Studs. 1997. *The Good War: An Oral History of World War II*. New York: New Press.

Tewksbury, Donald G. 1965. *The Founding of American Colleges and Universities before the Civil War*. [Hamden, CT]: Archon Books.

Thelin, John R. 1982. *Higher Education and Its Useful Past: Applied History in Research and Planning*. Rochester, VT: Schenkman.

———. 2004a. "Higher Education and the Public Trough: A Historical Perspective." In *Public Funding of Higher Education: Changing Contexts and New Rationales*, edited by Edward St. John and Michael D. Parsons, 21–39. Baltimore: Johns Hopkins University Press.

———. 2004b. *A History of American Higher Education*. Baltimore: Johns Hopkins University Press.

Thorne, Barrie. 1973. "Professional Education in Law." In *Education for the Professions of Medicine, Law, Theology, and Social Welfare*, edited by Everett C. Hughes, Barrie Thorne, Agostino M. DeBaggis, Arnold Gurin, and David Williams, 101–68. New York: McGraw-Hill.

Times Higher Education Supplement. 2015. "World University Rankings 2014–15." Accessed August 4, 2015. https://www.timeshighereducation.co.uk/world-university-rankings/2015/world-ranking#/sort/o/direction/asc.

Trow, Martin. 1988. "American Higher Education: Past, Present, and Future." *Educational Researcher* 7 (3): 13–23.

———. 1999. "From Mass Higher Education to Universal Access: The American Advantage." *Minerva* 37:303–28.

Turner, Ralph. 1960. "Sponsored and Contest Mobility and the School System." *American Sociological Review* 25:855–67.

Tyack, David, and Cuban, Larry. 1995. *Tinkering toward Utopia: Reflections on a Century of Public School Reform*. Cambridge, MA: Harvard University Press.

University of California Data Analysis. 2014. "UC Funding and Fees Analysis." Accessed September 2, 2014. http://ucpay.globl.org/funding_vs_fees.php.

University of California Office of the President. 2015. "California Freshman Admissions for 2014." Last modified May 16, 2016. http://www.ucop.edu/news/factsheets/fa112014adm.html.

University of California, Berkeley. 2015. "By the Numbers." Accessed April 28, 2015. http://www.berkeley.edu/about/bythenumbers.

University of Virginia 2014. "Financing the University 101." Last modified February 22, 2013. http://www.virginia.edu/finance101/answers.html.

U.S. Bureau of the Census. 1975. *Historical Statistics of the United States: Colonial Times to 1970*. Washington, DC: Government Printing Office.

U.S. Department of Education. 1993. *120 Years of American Education: A Statistical Portrait*. Washington, DC: Government Printing Office.

U.S. News and World Report. 2015a. "Best Grad Schools." Accessed April 28, 2015. http://grad-schools.usnews.rankingsandreviews.com/best-graduate-schools.

———. 2015b. "How U.S. News Calculated the 2015 Best Colleges Rankings." Accessed April 28, 2015. http://www.usnews.com/education/best-colleges/articles/2014/09/08/how-us-news-calculated-the-2015-best-colleges-rankings.

———. 2015c. "National Universities Rankings." Accessed April 28, 2015. http://colleges.usnews.rankingsandreviews.com/best-colleges/rankings/national-universities.

———. 2015d. "Top 100 Lowest Acceptance Rates." Accessed April 27, 2015. http://colleges.usnews.rankingsandreviews.com/best-colleges/rankings/lowest-acceptance-rate.

Veysey, Laurence S. 1970. *The Emergence of the American University*. Chicago: University of Chicago Press.

Wai, Jonathan. 2013. "Investigating America's Elite: Cognitive Ability, Education, and Sex Differences." *Intelligence* 41:203–11. http://www.sciencedirect.com/science /article/pii/S0160289613000263.

Warrell, Helen, and John Authers. 2014. "Cambridge University Seeks to Emulate US Ivy League Fundraising." *Financial Times*, January 26. http://www.ft.com/intl/cms /s/0/f2e4d1ec-8671-11e3-aa31-00144feab7de.html#axzz4AozIsQ2w.

Weber, Max. 1978. *Economy and Society*. Berkeley: University of California Press.

Webometrics Ranking of World Universities. 2014. "Top 2000 Universities by Google Scholar Citations." Accessed June 11, 2014. http://www.webometrics.info.

Weissmann, Jordan. 2013. "The Ever-Shrinking Role of Tenured College Professors (in 1 Chart)." *Atlantic*. April 10. http://www.theatlantic.com/business/archive/2013 /04/the-ever-shrinking-role-of-tenured-college-professors-in-1-chart/274849/.

Zumeta, William. 2004. "State Higher Education Financing: Demand Imperatives Meet Structural, Cyclical, and Political Constraints." In *Public Funding of Higher Education: Changing Contexts and New Rationales*, edited by Edward St. John and Michael D. Parsons, 79–107. Baltimore: Johns Hopkins University Press.

INDEX

Abbott, Andrew, 81

Academic Charisma and the Origins of the Research University (Clark), 17, 20–21

admissions, 9, 114, 133, 159–61, 163–65, 168–69, 173, 175, 182

Afghanistan, 155

Albany (New York), 31

American Academy of Arts and Sciences, 160

American Association for the Advancement of Science, 204–5n8

American Association of Universities (AAU), 90, 160, 170–71

American Dream, 104, 181, 194

American higher education, 40, 109, 128, 135, 176–77, 179–80, 182; academic principle, acting on, 193; access, broadening of, 97–98, 103, 105, 108, 149–50, 162–63; as adaptable enterprise, 1, 42–43, 188; admissions process, 163–65, 168–69; ambiguity of, 185–86; anarchic complexity of, 193–94; as anomaly, 1; anxiety, generating of, 167–69; as autonomous, 1; broad array of constituencies, 184; capacity for accomplishment of, 58; capacity in place, 41; charismatic authority in, 187; during Cold War, 141, 144–50, 155; community, as extension of, 43; consumer orientation of, 68–69, 97–98, 143; consumer sensitivity of, 42, 74, 80, 92–93, 98–100, 149, 183–84; content of, as more liberal, 92; as contest mobility, 79, 92; contradiction, thriving on, 71, 195; credentialism, rise of, 93, 98; criticism of, 181; cultural capital, 82, 127; curriculum content of, 75–77; curriculum inertia, 80; as decentralized, 1; defining traits of, 183–88; development of, 2, 189–90; disaggregation, promotion of, 192–93; distinctiveness of, 87; diversity of choices, 164, 166; economic capital, 82;

as elite, 184–85; entrepreneurial autonomy of, 5, 19, 183; as essential, 60; expansion of, 89; fluidity of, 165; formalism of, 80, 93; free speech, preserving of, 188; government spending on, 156–57; as hierarchical, 12; humble origins of, 1; and hypocrisy, 193; insider knowledge, rewarding of, 165; institutional autonomy, 183; institutional stratification of, 5; and logrolling, 193; market orientation of, 6–8, 18, 21, 42, 74, 80, 82, 114, 132, 142, 144, 149, 158, 182; mean, regression to, 142; organizational anarchy of, 190, 196; organizational complexity of, 186–88; paradox of, 138–39, 188–91; pecking order of, 80–86; peculiarities of, 2; political pressure, 98–99; popular culture, as part of, 65–66; populism, and elitism, balancing act between, 115; as populist, 43, 184; practicality of, 43–44, 91–92, 184, 185; as private good, 72, 87, 92, 95, 98, 100, 142–44, 149, 155, 158, 195; private-sector growth, 113, 117; professional, and liberal, shift from, 72–75, 78, 81–82, 92; professional education, 91; professional hypocrisy of, 190; prototype of, 142; as public good, 71–72, 87, 92, 95, 98, 100, 142–43, 146, 150–51, 155, 158, 195; public investment in, 141; public inscrutability of, 190; public and private education, mingling of, 129–39; public and private universities, unclear distinction between, 110–11; reform proposals, threat of, 181, 191–96; rational authority in, 187; relative autonomy of, 189; selectivity of, 159–60; sensitivity to consumers, 183–84; social advantage, providing of, 166, 168–69; social capital, 82, 127; socialization, as mechanism for, 98, 100; social mobility, 88, 167–68; state control, partial autonomy from, 74; stratification of, 80–86, 96–98, 107–8, 114, 159–60, 162;